The Beginner's Guide to Bonsai

The Beginner's Guide to Bonsai

Ken Norman

with photographs by
Peter Stiles

ABBEYDALE PRESS

This paperback edition published in 2006 by
Abbeydale Press
An imprint of
Bookmart Limited
Registered Number 2372865
Trading as Bookmart Limited
Blaby Road
Wigston
Leicestershire
LE18 4SE

ISBN 1-86147-181-5

10 9 8 7 6 5 4 3 2 1

Copyright © 2004 Bookmart Limited

All rights reserved. No part of this publication may be reproduced, stored in a retrieval system or transmitted by any means, electronic, mechanical, or otherwise, without the prior permission of the publisher.

Printed in Dubai

Designed, packaged and produced for Bookmart by Stonecastle Graphics Limited

Text by Ken Norman
Photography by Peter Stiles
Designed by Paul Turner and Sue Pressley
Edited by Philip de Ste. Croix

Author's Acknowledgements
The author would like to thank his wife Ann for her invaluable assistance with writing and proof reading, Jane and Robin Loder at Leonardslee Gardens for their cooperation, and Hannah Pratt as hand model for the step-by-step photography.

Additional pictures:
Ken Norman: pages 10, 14, 15, 39 (left).
Bill Jordan: pages 60, 61 (centre, below left and below right).

Details of main bonsai specimens shown on the following pages:

Page 1:
Acer palmatum 'Nomura'
Japanese maple
Style: Informal Upright
Height: 66cm (26in)
Pot: English; Gordon Duffett
Approximate age: 50 years

Page 2:
Acer palmatum
Japanese maple
Style: Clump
Height: 58cm (23in)
Pot: English; Bryan Albright
Approximate age: 35 years

Page 3:
Acer palmatum 'Kyohime'
Japanese maple
Style: Clump
Height: 41cm (16in)
Pot: English; Derek Aspinall
Approximate age: 45 years

Page 6:
Acer palmatum 'Deshojo'
Japanese maple
Style: Informal Upright
Height: 81cm (32in)
Pot: English; Derek Aspinall
Approximate age: 50 years

Page 22:
Lonicera pileata
Honeysuckle
Style: Twin Trunk Informal Upright
Height: 43cm (17in)
Pot: Japanese
Approximate age: 20 years

Page 36:
Fagus sylvatica
European beech
Style: Ripple Trunk
Height: 105cm (41in)
Pot: English; Ken Potter
Approximate age: 35 years

Page 62:
Chamaecyparis pisifera
Sawara cypress
Style: Informal Upright
Height: 63cm (25in)
Pot: English; Derek Aspinall
Approximate age: 90 years

Page 72:
Larix leptolepis
Japanese larch
Style: Driftwood
Height: 55cm (21in)
Pot: English slate
Approximate age: 22 years

Page 90:
Rhododendron obtusum 'Amoenum'
Kirishima azalea
Style: Slanting
Height: 86cm (34in)
Pot: English; Derek Aspinall
Approximate age: 75 years

Page 92:
Acer palmatum 'Deshojo'
Japanese maple
Style: Informal Upright
Height: 71cm (28in)
Pot: English; Derek Aspinall
Approximate age: 55 years

Page 93:
Acer buergerianum
Trident maple
Style: Informal Upright
Height: 69cm (27in)
Pot: Japanese
Approximate age: 35 years

Page 94:
Acer palmatum 'Ukon'
Japanese maple
Style: Twin Trunk
Height: 84cm (33in)
Pot: English; Denis O'Neil
Approximate age: 45 years

Page 95:
Ulmus procera
English elm
Style: Informal Upright
Height: 66cm (26in)
Pot: English; Bryan Albright
Approximate age: 70 years

Contents

Introduction 6

What is Bonsai? 10
The History of Bonsai 12
Traditional Bonsai 14
Trees and Shrubs for Bonsai 16
Basic Styles 18
More Advanced Styles 20

Getting Started 22
Bonsai Basics 24
Propagation from Seed 26
Propagation from Cuttings 27
Tools for Potting 28
Tools for Wiring 29
Pots and Containers 30
Preparing Pots 32
Soil and Composts 34

General Techniques 36
Seasonal Maintenance 38
Branch Pruning 40
Defoliating 42
Clip and Grow 44
Pruning for Shape 46
Wiring 48

Root Pruning 50
Repotting 52
Watering 54
Feeding 56
Regular Maintenance 58
Pests and Diseases 60

Creating a Bonsai 62
European Olive 64
Bigleaf Podocarp 66
Japanese Maple 68
Weeping Fig 70

Advanced Techniques 72
Layering 74
Grafting 76
Planting a Forest or Group 78
Rock Planting 82
Creating Jin 84
Creating Sharimiki 87
Collecting from the Wild 88

Specimen Bonsai 90

Index 96

Introduction

The word 'bonsai' basically means a plant, tree or group of trees or plants growing in a container.

The art of growing a bonsai lies in being able to select a plant or tree that has the potential of becoming a bonsai and cultivating it with care using general horticultural techniques. These techniques, many of which are refined for bonsai growing, are then combined with artistic expression, so that the plant blends with its container to give a true impression of a mature tree, but in miniature form.

The beauty of a mature bonsai relies on the harmony between the tree and its pot. A bonsai in a compatible container can be likened to a classical work of art mounted in a similarly sympathetic frame. The viewer, in both cases, should be drawn to look at the main subject, be it the bonsai tree or the work of art. Although the pot or frame is of secondary importance, it should exist as a total part of the composition and the whole arrangement in each case should be pleasing to the eye.

Introduction

To get started in practising the art and culture of bonsai you will probably need a little bit of gardening knowledge, a dash of common sense and the desire to succeed. If you already grow plants or trees in containers, you may already have mastered some basic techniques required for bonsai culture. You may have purchased a bonsai from a supermarket, garden centre or bonsai nursery and have experienced mixed success in keeping the tree healthy, or even in looking like a tree at all. If this is the case, then some practical advice could help you to develop the skills necessary to achieve good results. Acquiring these skills will inevitably improve your understanding of the subject and therefore the quality of your final product.

Purchasing a 'ready-made' bonsai is often the first step into a hobby that could well become an obsession. Bonsai is about creating miniature versions of mature trees, using the same materials from which the full-size trees are grown. The tree is a part of an entire composition, the other element being the pot or container. Both tree and container must complement one another in shape, size and colour, just as a frame complements a beautiful painting.

The techniques used to produce bonsai are simply the application of normal horticultural processes that are used to grow and shape trees. They may be modified slightly to suit the art of bonsai, but anyone should be able to achieve satisfactory results fairly quickly.

Right: The art of bonsai is all about creating miniature versions of mature trees that would grow to many metres in height in their natural habitats. This specimen is Acer palmatum.

Introduction 9

Left: Part of the author's impressive bonsai collection at Leonardslee Gardens, near Horsham, West Sussex.

Left: Bonsai may be grown as single specimens, groups or even small forests of miniature trees. This is a group of Carpinus laxiflora.

Chapter 1

What is Bonsai?

Bonsai specimens can be almost any size, ranging from about 2.5cm (1in) high to plants as large as can reasonably be carried by two or more people. Most people tend to grow small or medium-sized bonsai, but when the fascination develops into an obsession, one tends to want to grow larger and larger trees as there seems to be much more scope to develop ideas. It is important not to be too ambitious too soon, but to move forward slowly and in logical steps, so that the techniques employed in bonsai culture remain with you for future reference.

This art form can also be very therapeutic as it can demand many hours, weeks or even months of quiet study of trees, both full size and miniature, to understand their growth patterns and potential. Close examination of the natural structure and development of full-size trees will bring new impetus to understanding the design concepts of bonsai and the inspiration to look more closely at this most rewarding living art form. A full-size tree may have hundreds of branches, but when developing a bonsai that is only 30-50cm (12-20in) in height a very much smaller number of branches, perhaps only nine or ten, will have to convey the same impression of size, but in miniature. Therefore close study of full-size trees plays a very important part in the learning process.

The History of Bonsai

Bonsai is thought to have originated in China some 1500-2000 years ago. Penjing is the word that is used to describe the Chinese version of bonsai and this discipline seems to cover a wide range of horticultural styles including rock plantings and tray landscapes.

Bonsai appears to be something of a mystery to many people but early records show that bonsai, or penjing, has been grown in China for over 2000 years, and in Japan there are records going back some 1300 years which include descriptions and drawings of bonsai, as well as woodblock prints and screens.

During the Chin dynasty (221-206BC) China and Japan began to make contact when Buddhism was introduced via Korea. It seems that many Buddhist priests were instrumental in encouraging the ceremonial use of potted plants. As with many other things, the people of Japan seem to be extremely good at recognizing the potential of something, whether it is cameras, cars or bonsai. They then develop and improve the product until it virtually reaches perfection. Bonsai is the product we are interested in and the Japanese have made a particularly good job of developing this into a recognized and flourishing art form.

Early bonsai were almost certainly trees collected from the mountainous regions of China or Japan. These were naturally stunted trees that were carefully collected, planted into containers, usually ceramic ones, and displayed in or around the collectors' homes. Nature would have ravaged these trees and contorted them into extremely interesting shapes.

One of the earliest pieces of documentation in Japan appears in a picture scroll of 1195 called the Saigyo Momogatari Emaki. Saigyo was a priest and this scroll depicts a potted plant as an important symbol of his status. Other early mentions of bonsai in Japan appear in the records of the Kasuga Shrine that were made during the Kamakura period of 1192-1333 and in scrolls dating back to the Heian period of 794-1191 that show scenes of domestic activities that include bonsai displayed in and around homes. There are drawings from the same period that provide clear evidence of bonsai being cultivated around this time. This suggests that the culture of bonsai growing existed in Japan as early as 1300 years ago.

Bonsai became increasingly popular in the late nineteenth century using very much improved techniques and many growers began to produce commercial versions of these fascinating miniature trees. Bonsai was introduced to the Japan Society of London in 1901 and bonsai plants were mentioned in Cassell's *Encyclopedia of Gardening* in 1905. A collection of bonsai seems to have been housed at Windsor Castle in 1907 and the first bonsai exhibition in London was in 1909.

Below: By creating your own bonsai you are continuing a tradition that has been practised for 2000 years. It is not surprising that bonsai is popular, as it combines artistic ability and gardening skills in equal measure.

Exhibitions also took place in Paris and other major cities and caused considerable excitement wherever they were seen. Over the past 50 years these small trees have become popular throughout the world and it would be difficult to find a country where there is no interest in this living art form.

There are now many local, national and international bonsai societies that work together for the advancement of bonsai culture worldwide, and a number of excellent nurseries that specialize in bonsai growing as well as wholesale and retail operations.

Belonging to a bonsai club or society will enable most people to achieve much more than they would by working alone. Within any society there will many people who are only too willing to divulge their 'secrets' and help beginners to progress in a steady fashion. There are actually no secrets in the bonsai world, as you will find as you learn to develop your skills.

Above: An illustration by Ella Du Cane for The Flowers and Gardens of Japan, *published in 1908 by A & C Black. In the bottom right of the painting can be seen an Informal Upright Pine Bonsai.*

Below: This woodblock print by Katsukawa Shunsen ga, circa 1820, depicts a scene from Chushingura Drama. The print shows a potted plum tree which is typical of those used as decorative plants in that period.

Traditional Bonsai

Traditional bonsai are normally seen as beautiful artistic creations but some can be a little bit too contorted or artificial looking for some tastes. It should be appreciated that bonsai can be considered an illusion as currently it is an almost totally controlled product from start to finish. There is no true finish to bonsai, of course, as they need to be cared for correctly for the whole of their lives. If this is not done, the trees can lose their defined shape completely within a very short time.

Bonsai range in size from no more than 2.5cm (1in) up to about 1.25m (4ft) but there is no prescribed limit. They are generally classified into three categories.

The first and smallest size is known as 'mame', pronounced 'ma-mey'. These tiny trees can vary in size from just a few centimetres up to about 15cm (6in) in height.

The next size is normally known as 'shohin', pronounced 'sho-hin', and these can be anything from 15-30cm (6-12in) in height.

Bigger trees

From about 30cm (12in) upward in size the trees are just known as bonsai. Sometimes they are so large that it takes two or three people to lift them. These larger trees are relatively easy to look after, as they are generally grown in quite large pots.

This means that the watering situation may not be as critical as it is with the mame or shohin, which can be grown in very small pots, and so in need of more frequent watering.

Traditional bonsai as we know it began in the latter part of the nineteenth century when interest in bonsai widened and growers began to produce trees on a commercial basis. Various styles were classified and the training techniques began to be formalized and developed into those that are commonly used today.

These pages contain a number of images of traditional Japanese bonsai taken at some famous bonsai collections in Japan during the author's visits to this fascinating country.

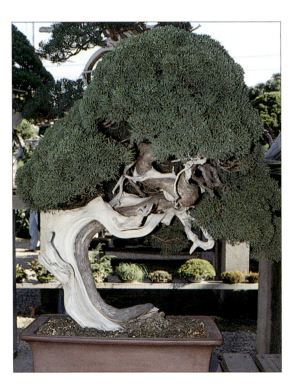

Below: A Chinese juniper grown in the Informal Upright Driftwood Style. This is a superb example of this type of bonsai showing the complex and beautiful trunk leading to the rich green clouds of foliage.

Below right: An Informal Upright Japanese white pine with a superb trunk taper that gives the tree a feeling of great age. The branch placement and overall design make this a very traditional style bonsai.

What is Bonsai?

Above left: A Chinese juniper in Driftwood Style with a spectacular trunk that rises up through the main foliage areas. This famous tree has been shown at many exhibitions throughout Japan.

Above: The excellent trunk buttress, surface roots and branch structure on this Informal Upright Japanese maple make this a fine example of this type of traditional Japanese bonsai.

Left: A Japanese white pine Semi-Cascade bonsai. This magnificent, well-balanced tree is planted in a suitably deep pot that complements the excellent trunk and branch structure.

Trees and Shrubs for Bonsai

Almost any tree or shrub that has the potential to develop a substantial woody trunk of mature appearance may be suitable for growing as a bonsai.

Some trees, such as Japanese maples, elm and juniper, perform better than others because of their relatively small natural leaf size. Their leaf shape is also very suitable, while others, such as horse chestnut, sycamore and ash, are substantially more difficult to turn into bonsai. The latter naturally have quite large leaves, which makes it more difficult to obtain good leaf size reduction although this can be achieved with patience over quite a long period of time.

You should look for plants that have relatively small leaves or needles so that, when certain bonsai techniques are used, they will produce even smaller leaves and needles as the plant matures.

These are examples of the type of plants that can be purchased from a garden centre before any bonsai styling is carried out.

Podocarpus

Ficus benjamina 'Bushy King'

Further examples of good material for bonsai are beech, hornbeam, azalea, cotoneaster, box, pine, larch, cryptomeria and some of the small-leaved varieties of honeysuckle. There are so many possibilities that it is impossible to name them all here so it is important to know which are the best for getting started.

If you would like to have some flowering or fruiting bonsai in your collection, you will need to acquire material that has naturally small flowers and fruit. This is very important to remember because the flowers and fruit on any plant will not reduce in size, as the leaves do.

The basic criteria are that each piece of material can be shaped, using the various methods described later, and then planted into a complementary container so that it represents a full-size, mature tree, but in miniature.

What is Bonsai? 17

Acer palmatum
(Japanese maple)

Juniperus chinensis *'Blaaws'*

Buxus sempervirens

Basic Styles

Informal Upright

This is a very common bonsai style in which the trunk is upright but not absolutely straight. It is one of the most popular styles, probably because full-size mature trees often conform to this shape. By observing full-size trees in nature, you will soon get a good idea of how trees grow and into which styles your bonsai may fit.

The root base should be examined closely, as with every bonsai styling exercise, before any other work is carried out. The tree should be carefully studied and its best side decided upon. It may be that it is better viewed from a totally different angle to its original placement in the pot. Quite often it is possible to style an Informal Upright tree by just using pruning techniques and without using any wire at all.

Once you have chosen the best angle from which to view the tree, you can then begin the work of shaping your bonsai to suit this style.

All bonsai have a best viewing angle, which is usually referred to as the front of the tree. However, remember that every bonsai should look good from all angles.

Twin or Multi-Trunk

When tree seeds germinate naturally very close to one another they often grow up together and form an arrangement of two trees, which in bonsai is referred to as Twin Trunk. Several seeds may germinate close together and form multi-trunk trees and these all fit into one of the many bonsai styles. As they grow larger, the distance between them becomes smaller until eventually

Below left: Acer palmatum *'Deshojo' – an example of an Informal Upright style.*

Below: This Twin Trunk bonsai is an Acer palmatum *'Ukon'.*

they appear as a single tree apparently with two trunks or more.

This can be achieved in bonsai either by planting two or more trees very close together or by beginning with a plant that already has two or more trunks. If you plan to begin with two separate trees, they can be tied together at their bases so that as they develop, they tend to grow together as one tree, albeit with two or more trunks.

It is always better to start with two plants of the same species and variety and with trunks of differing sizes. In other words one should have a taller and fatter trunk than the other. If a natural twin is available, it will need to have two differently sized trunks.

The smaller trunk should be arranged so that it grows alongside the main trunk but slightly to the rear of that trunk. It is important that the two trunks bases are adjacent to each other.

Slanting

The Slanting style can have its trunk leaning to one side by as much as 60 degrees. This bonsai style is based on natural trees that have been affected by stormy weather, and which have been blown over at an angle. The natural reaction of the tree after this has happened is to redirect its branch growth to suit the new growing angle of the trunk.

The basic steps described previously to ascertain the trunk angle and root structure should be followed so that the angle of the trunk looks as natural as possible. The position of the branches must relate to the trunk so that a satisfactory mature shape is obtained.

Where a branch has to be placed in a drooping position, make sure that at the junction of the branch with the trunk it bends down immediately it leaves the trunk.

When styling a bonsai from scratch, make sure that all branches are positioned as you want them, including the smallest twigs. Attention to this type of detail in the early stages of styling can make or break the appearance of the end product.

Left: This superb Rhododendron obtusum 'Amoenum' is beautifully balanced in a Slanting style.

More Advanced Styles

Right: This Juniperus chinensis *(Chinese juniper), Cascade is positioned correctly with the main trunk cascading over the corner of the pot and down across the front.*

Semi-Cascade

The Semi-Cascade style reflects the effect of extreme growing conditions on a tree. This style of bonsai is designed to give the appearance of a very old tree growing from the side of a quarry or rock face.

Although the trunk line may have initially been upright, it would, in natural conditions, have been bent over into a roughly horizontal position by continuously falling rocks, stones or soil.

Following the initial steps when assessing any bonsai style as already described, ascertain the root structure and trunk line.

This distinctive style is normally identified when a bonsai leans over beyond about 60 degrees to one side or the other and even down to as low as horizontal, or even a little below the rim of the pot.

If it drops over the edge of the pot and down the side, it is then described as a Cascade.

Below: Semi-Cascade pyracantha.

Cascade

Just like the Semi-Cascade style, the trunk line of this style of bonsai begins by growing up from the soil level before cascading over and down the side of the pot.

Once again this style represents a tree that has been growing in very difficult circumstances, perhaps out of the side of a rock face or in a similarly severe habitat.

This style is not one of the easiest to produce and beginners should be aware that it is normally considered an advanced project if one is aiming to achieve a top quality result.

Literati

This is a rather unusual style in that it does not conform to the usual rules that are observed when styling bonsai trees. It normally has a very tall, slim, freestyle trunk, quite often with very little taper, ending in a small number of branches on the upper part of the tree.

Examples of this style in the wild are very common and can be seen where very old, tall pines have discarded their lower branches and are left with just a few at the apex.

The trunk is very important. It is never straight and should be full of character. When choosing a tree that may be suitable for use as a Literati style bonsai, you will need to find a piece of material that may have been neglected or damaged, or both, and that is virtually unsuitable for anything else.

Conifers, particularly pines, make the best Literati bonsai, and it is these same species of tree that seem to exhibit this style when growing naturally in the wild.

Pots for this style of bonsai should be circular and not too large, as this will overpower the appearance of the tree. Pots with a primitive, rather rough appearance will suit this style of bonsai admirably.

If the branches are made to droop severely, the effect of considerable age can be achieved.

Above: Often a neglected or damaged plant, such as this European larch, may be transformed into a Literati style bonsai.

Left: The trunk of this Japanese larch has the appearance of a piece of weathered driftwood.

Driftwood

Driftwood style is so called because the main trunk is reminiscent of a piece of water-washed and bleached driftwood. Root over Rock, Root on Rock and Root in Rock are very much self-explanatory styles and require a bit more patience to achieve than most of the other styles.

In fact there are so many variations and personal interpretations that can be incorporated into bonsai styling, that it is really impossible to list them all.

Styles and variations

There are many other styles and variations of the main styles mentioned previously and so there is scope for experimentation on an infinite variety of shapes and sizes that will make very acceptable bonsai.

Chapter 2
Getting Started

The first step to get you started is to acquire some general knowledge of gardening techniques as well as a feel for the way plants react to various actions. The latter skill will probably be picked up quite quickly with experience as you progress through this book.

You may buy a tree that appears to be finished but do beware, because your newly acquired tree, if looked after well, can grow quickly and soon lose its shape. You will get good advice, when buying, if you go to a good bonsai dealer, but other bonsai outlets may not offer any advice at all. Check that any tree that you intend to buy is firm in its pot. If not, then it means that it has recently been repotted or has a poor root system. The tree may have training wire on its branches, but if it is not cutting into the wood, it should be all right. Do not be afraid to question the supplier because the more you know about your tree the more chance you have of keeping it growing successfully.

Bonsai Basics

You will need to decide what type of bonsai you are thinking of growing. Will you keep it indoors or outdoors? Check that the tree you select is suitable for the environment in which it is going to be kept.

The place where you live will determine the varieties of trees that can be kept indoors or outdoors. Trees or plants that naturally grow outdoors in your locality are the ones that are suitable for outdoor bonsai. Those that come from different climatic conditions will need to be grown indoors or at least in a more controlled environment.

Training, styling and maintenance techniques are the same for indoor and outdoor bonsai, but the environmental conditions that need to be maintained will be very different.

In temperate areas indoor trees need to be kept in warmer, more humid conditions, which is not easy in modern centrally heated homes. They need good light but should not be placed where they can receive direct sunlight through a window, as this will quickly scorch the leaves and could lead to the death of the tree. Soil should be kept moist at all times but never waterlogged, as the tree will drown leading to root rot and ultimately rapid death.

Standing the pot on a shallow tray filled with gravel or absorbent granules can increase the humidity around an indoor bonsai. This should then be kept moist at all times. This allows the water to evaporate slowly and drift up and around the foliage. This slows down the transpiration of water from the foliage and will help to keep the tree healthy.

If you are going to grow outdoor trees that are suitable for your climate, then you will find that the conditions will probably take care of themselves, but you will still have monitor those conditions on a daily basis.

Below: It is a good idea to make a collection of suitable bonsai pots from which to choose before you start growing a specimen.

To get going on some real bonsai work you will need a certain amount of equipment. This includes basic tools, a few pots, some bonsai wire and some other bits and pieces, such as plastic mesh and an old toothbrush.

To begin you do not need to spend a lot of money on expensive bonsai tools when you can make do with a pair of general-purpose scissors, secateurs, wire cutters and chopsticks. You will eventually progress towards purchasing better quality Japanese bonsai tools as they make a much better job of bonsai cultivation because they are designed for each specific purpose. More detailed advice about the use of tools is dealt with as we progress through the book.

Above: This group of newly trained bonsai are being grown outside on the windowsill. You need to choose plants that are hardy and suitable for the conditions in your own garden if you are to grow outdoor varieties successfully.

Left: The soil should be kept moist at all times and never be allowed to dry out. This is a typical example of an indoor bonsai.

Propagation from Seed

One of the first ways to get started in bonsai growing is to grow plants from seed, although this can can be quite tedious and slow. If you grow from seed, you will always know the exact age of your tree, which is probably one of the first questions you will be asked about any of your bonsai trees.

Make sure that any seeds you purchase are fresh and that you choose seeds that will produce plants with naturally small leaves or needles. If your chosen seeds have a hard case, they will probably need to be cracked, chipped or stratified to aid germination. To crack the seeds you will need to squeeze them gently with pliers until the hard seed coat cracks. This will let in moisture to the kernel and aid germination. Chipping seeds is done by carefully cutting a small chip from the seed coat, which serves the same purpose as cracking the seed. Stratifying means that you should mix the seeds with a small amount of moist peat or sand in a covered container, and place it in the salad compartment of a refrigerator, not a freezer, for three to four weeks before sowing them. This again helps to break the dormancy of the seeds and speeds up germination.

This process usually takes place naturally when seeds either remain on trees or fall to the ground during winter.

You will need a seed tray or flowerpot and a bag of seed compost to begin your journey into the fascinating world of bonsai.

The seed tray or pot needs to be almost filled with the seed compost which is then gently flattened but not compressed. If the seeds are fairly large, you will need to place them carefully at regular intervals on the surface of the compost. They are then covered with a further layer of compost, which should be made no deeper than the size of the seeds themselves.

Gently firm this top layer of soil before watering from a can that has a fine rose attached to the spout. At this point you should also spray the soil with a fungicide to guard against any sort of fungal attack.

Cover the completed tray of seeds with a seed tray cover to retain some warmth and humidity and place it in a greenhouse until the seeds show signs of germination. At this point, and if you wish, you can place them on an outdoor bench and remove the cover. Keep a watchful eye on your new, young, precious plants, for they are liable to attack from all sorts of creatures. Slugs, snails and a variety of insects may take a liking to your plants and they could make a tasty meal for something overnight.

When propagating from seed, you may find that some tree varieties, especially Japanese maples, produce variable results. This, in many cases, serves to enhance your collection of trees because you will enjoy a large variety of interesting leaf shapes and colours.

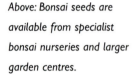

Above: Bonsai seeds are available from specialist bonsai nurseries and larger garden centres.

Below: Place the seeds individually onto the compost in neat rows.

Below left: Cover the seeds with a layer of compost to the same depth as the size of the seed.

Below: Water well following sowing.

Propagation from Cuttings

A slightly quicker route to enter into the world of bonsai is to produce suitable plants from cuttings. To achieve a speedier result, and to produce plants that have the same characteristics as the parent plant, you will need to propagate from cuttings.

This entails taking small shoots from a larger plant of your choice and planting them in suitable cutting compost that enables them to produce roots. Hardwood and softwood cuttings are the two types normally used when propagating woody plants for bonsai. You will need to take softwood, or even semi-ripe, cuttings in late spring or early summer, and hardwood cuttings in the autumn. Again you will need a seed tray but this time you should use cutting compost which generally has more grit in the mix.

An alternative to commercially available cutting compost is Akadama, a soil from Japan which is described in more detail in the soil section. This is an excellent medium for encouraging healthy root production.

For broadleaf trees, take a cutting that has several nodes and cut off the lowest leaves and the growing tip. If the leaves are fairly large, cut off about two-thirds of the actual leaf using sharp scissors. This reduces the rate at which the cutting will lose water by transpiration through its leaves. Since two-thirds of each leaf has been removed, then it is fair to say that the transpiration rate is decreased by two-thirds.

For conifers, take heel cuttings by pulling down on the shoot until it becomes detached. Once again reduce the amount of foliage but leave some in place as in the case of most conifers the cutting will die without any foliage.

Having filled a tray with a suitable soil make a small hole for each cutting using a chopstick or similar implement.

Insert the cuttings into the compost to about one third of their length, and when the tray is full, water as with seeds. As a precaution against fungal attack, spray with a fungicide immediately.

Cover the tray to retain humidity and place it in a cool shady situation.

Cuttings from broadleaf trees

Left: Remove about two-thirds of the leaves of broadleaf cuttings to slow down the rate of transpiration of moisture from them. This aids the cuttings when they are producing roots.

Left: Make holes with a chopstick and insert the broadleaf cuttings into potting compost in a seed tray.

Cuttings from conifers

Above: Tear the required shoot from the stock plant so that a 'heel' remains on the cutting.

Above: Make holes with a chopstick and insert the conifer cuttings into potting compost in a seed tray.

Tools for Potting

The most commonly used tool for bonsai potting and repotting processes is a rake/spatula. If you purchase a genuine Japanese item, you will be asked to pay a considerable sum of money but you can make a simple substitute for this by using an old dinner fork, which has half the length of the prongs bent over at about 90 degrees to form a simple rake.

Also required is a pair of scissors for trimming the fine roots, a heavy-duty pair of scissors for cutting heavier roots and a chopstick for working the soil into and around the roots when carrying out the potting process.

Another useful item is a root hook, which consists of a handle which has a single steel or brass hook attached. This tool is ideal for separating out congested and tangled root systems. Finally a coco brush or something similar is most useful for brushing the soil surface evenly when finishing off a repotting session.

Single root hooks are useful for untangling congested roots.

General purpose shears are ideal for pruning leaves or small branches.

A coco brush.

A rake/spatula is used for raking soil from roots when repotting and flattening soil following potting.

Ordinary bamboo or plastic chopsticks make ideal tools for working soil into roots when potting.

Metal sieves are used for grading soil particles to achieve a fine compost.

Getting Started 29

Tools for Wiring

There are three main tools required for the process of wiring a bonsai.

The first and most useful is a pair of wire cutters. These are available in a variety of sizes, usually small, medium and large, and again can be fairly expensive if you are buying the genuine Japanese article. However, you can do just as good a job with an ordinary pair of electrician's wire cutters that may be purchased at a much lower price. The main difference is that the Japanese versions have longer handles in proportion to the cutting blades than the electrician's version. This makes it very much easier to cut through thicker wire than with the electrician's wire cutters.

A pair of pliers is also a very useful part of the wiring toolkit. These would normally be jinning pliers, which double up here for holding and bending thicker gauges of wire. Jinning pliers are normally used as shown in the section relating to the forming of jin but they are a very useful general-purpose bonsai item to add to your bonsai toolkit and will also be needed when repotting, as shown in more detail in the potting section of this book. Quite often, when the wire reaches the end of a branch it may need to be bent sharply to finish off at the end to secure the branch within. Once again, a more economical alternative to the Japanese pliers is a standard pair of engineer's pliers.

A bonsai wire rack is a very useful and convenient dispenser for several different sizes of wire. In this example wires of seven different gauges are being stored neatly.

Left: These branches have been wired to help them retain their shapes when they are bent into more interesting positions.

Jinning pliers can be used for creating jin (see pages 84-87) as well as for other general uses.

Wire cutters are an essential part of every bonsai enthusiast's equipment.

Pots and Containers

The bonsai pot is not just the container in which to grow your bonsai. It is also most important that it blends well with the tree so that the final composition integrates well as a complementary unit.

Pots must be frost-proof if they are to be used for outdoor trees, and therefore should be made from stoneware. Pots made of other materials such as plastic and mica will also be fine, but they are best suited for use by beginners and as training pots. Most people graduate to stoneware pots eventually, as their visual impression gives the trees a far superior appearance.

You should make sure that the pots you choose have adequate drainage holes, usually quite large ones, so that excess water can drain away. Some pots may have a series of small holes around the perimeter of the base, which can be used to tie the tree into the pot. Check also that the base of the pot is flat so that there are no areas where water can become trapped.

All pots should have feet so that the base of the pot stands clear of the display stand. This allows for free airflow around the base of the pot, and will increase the chances of a healthy tree. Bonsai pots should be unglazed on the inside as this helps to keep the tree stable in the pot, especially when the roots have grown sufficiently to come into contact with the sides.

Bonsai pots are available in many different shapes, sizes and colours to suit all styles and species of plants, and a variety of examples are shown on these two pages.

In general, glazed or semi-glazed pots are most suitable for deciduous trees, and matt or unglazed pots are more complementary to conifers and evergreen trees. It must be pointed out that this is only a general rule and should be taken as a guideline. It should be remembered that the viewer's eye should be drawn to the base of the tree first, then the eye should be drawn up to view the main structure of the tree, with the pot being the last thing that you notice. However, the pot is still a very important part of the whole arrangement and therefore must complement the tree completely.

Semi-glazed rectangular pot

An unglazed handmade drum pot

Glazed rectangular pot

Getting Started 31

Glazed rectangular pot with rounded corners

Oval glazed pot

An unglazed rectangular pot

A glazed square cascade pot

An unglazed slip cast drum pot

Preparing Pots

All pots and containers should be cleaned and dried before repotting bonsai. When reusing pots, it is important to make sure that they have been thoroughly cleaned with a stiff brush using water to which has been added a small amount of washing-up liquid. The washing-up liquid will help to dislodge any stubborn dirty stains but remember to rinse well so as to dispel all traces of the detergent.

The drainage holes in the bottom of the pot should be covered with plastic mesh. This is used because it takes up almost no space in the pot and it will prevent any soil falling through the holes as well as stopping most unwanted pests from entering the soil through the holes.

The pieces of plastic mesh are held in place with what can be loosely described as a wire 'butterfly'. This is made by taking a short length of wire, carefully bending it into a loop at each end and then bending the two ends up at right angles. The two ends are then passed up through the holes and the mesh is placed over the two wire ends which are then bent over to secure the mesh over the holes. This is necessary because when the tree is placed into the pot, it will have to be moved around somewhat to settle it in place, which could result in the mesh moving away from the holes if it is not secured.

The final thing to do when preparing the pot is to pass a longer length of wire along the underside of the pot, thread the two ends up through the holes in the pot and pull it up tight. This piece of wire will then be used to secure the tree when it is placed into the pot.

Below: To prepare a pot for bonsai, first cut pieces of plastic mesh to cover the drainage holes in the pot. Make small wire 'butterflies' with which to anchor the mesh into the pot.

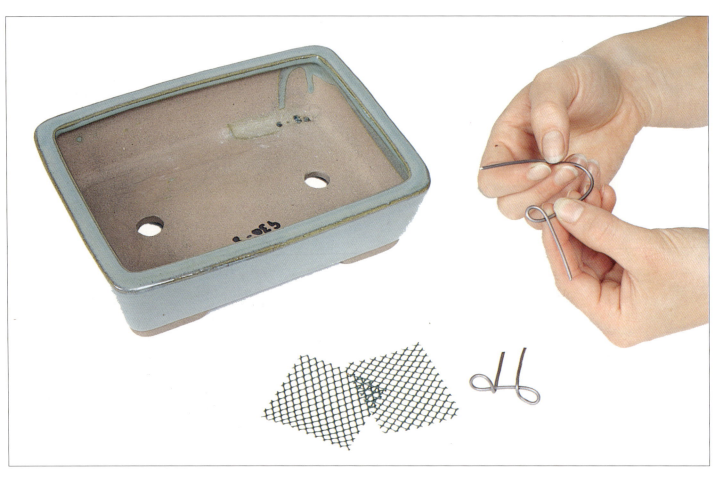

Getting Started

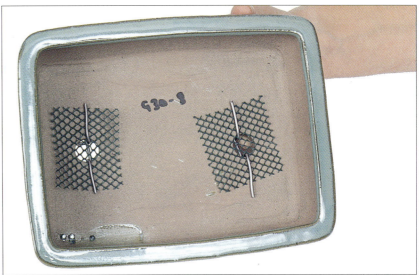

Above left: Fix the mesh into the pot using the small wire 'butterfly' anchors that you have made.

Above: Now the drainage mesh is secured in place over the holes in the pot.

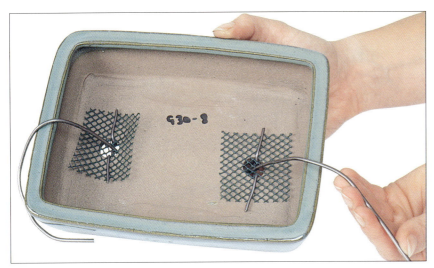

Above: Insert a length of wire through the two holes to use as a securing device which will help to keep the tree in place.

Right: Finally, spread a layer of soil evenly over the base of the pot.

Soil and Composts

It is possible to grow bonsai in almost any type of soil, but they will only remain healthy for a short time if the mix is not totally suitable.

A bonsai soil may be composed of just one ingredient or be a mix of two or three different ingredients. Needless to say, these must be of good quality if your bonsai is going to remain healthy and vibrant for many years to come.

The function of soil is to be able to hold sufficient water and nutrients, which in turn will give a regular supply of these to be absorbed by the roots of your tree.

The soil must not encourage root decay by storing too much water around the roots, but must allow excess water to drain away freely.

Free-draining soil is probably one of the most important materials used in the culture of bonsai. The soil must be open and contain as many air spaces as soil granules, as it is these air spaces that allow the root system to breathe.

The soil is also partly responsible for anchoring the tree into the pot and therefore should be substantial enough so that this can be achieved. In bonsai this is often assisted by tying the tree into the pot with wire.

An adequate general-purpose soil mix can be made up by combining one part of sphagnum moss peat, one part of loam and two parts of coarse sharp grit.

Search your local garden and DIY centres to find a suitable grit, as you will require one that has angular particles between 3mm and 6mm in size. Do not use grit that has very sharp slivers that may cause severe damage to roots when repotting. There are many varieties of grit available as well as many other suitable materials, that are ideal substitutes for grit, and these can be introduced into your soil mix as your experience in growing bonsai becomes more advanced.

Akadama

A mixture of loam, peat and grit

Coarse Akadama

Fine Akadama

Peat substitute

Kanuma

Smooth rounded grit

Coarse grit

Loam

Fine grit

Instead of loam, John Innes No.2 compost is also suitable but you should remember that this mix already has loam, grit and nutrients included in its composition.

Soil ingredients must be dry when mixed, and should pass through a sieve that allows the passage of particles of between 2mm and 6mm. Particles finer than this will block the air spaces in the soil and will be extremely detrimental to the root development of your tree.

Akadama, Kanuma and Kiryu

Other soils can be imported from Japan and these are available from good bonsai suppliers, but they are probably more suited to the experienced grower. If you are tempted, you will find that they provide superb growing conditions for many potted trees as well as many other types of plants.

There are three varieties available: Akadama, Kanuma and Kiryu. Akadama is a general-purpose soil and is suitable for most bonsai. Kanuma is particularly suitable for ericaceous plants such as azaleas, and Kiryu is best for pines and junipers but this is not normally easily available. These soils are generally more expensive than normal, easily obtainable ingredients. However, while they can be used neat they can also be mixed with peat and grit to make suitable mixtures that will help to keep the cost of soils to a minimum.

It is not recommended that you should mix fertilizers with the soil when potting your bonsai plants, but remember that you should add them as necessary at regular intervals throughout the growing season.

Feeding bonsai is dealt with in more detail later in this book.

Chapter 3
General Techniques

In early spring your trees will burst into action. Spring is the busiest time of the year as most trees will need root pruning and repotting just before the new growth begins. Should you experience severe frosts, protect repotted trees in a shed or cold greenhouse until the climatic conditions outside improve.

Pruning can be carried out in spring, when it is easy to see which twigs or branches need removing. Trimming trees in spring will get them in good shape for the new season. As shoots extend, cut back to one pair of leaves to maintain compact growth. Apply wire to conifers in the spring but not to deciduous trees. These are best dealt with in summer when they are more flexible. Make regular checks on trees that have been wired as it is surprising how rapidly the branches swell. If the wire is cutting into the bark, remove it immediately. Do not apply fertilizer to freshly potted trees as it can damage freshly pruned roots.

Seasonal Maintenance

You should have completed repotting by the beginning of summer. Trees will be well into growth, and shoots will need trimming regularly. Cut back deciduous shoots to one pair of leaves and pinch out conifer buds as they extend.

Water every day as the weather warms up and sometimes twice a day in very hot conditions. Never allow your bonsai trees to dry out. Feed your trees throughout spring and summer, but remember that the nitrogen level will need to be reduced into late summer.

The growth rate of trees slows down in autumn, and deciduous trees lose their leaves. Root growth slows down, and next season's buds begin to harden up for the winter. Continue to prune pines but not deciduous trees, as this could induce a spurt of late growth, which would be susceptible to frost damage. As growth slows right down, trimming of shoots will not be necessary. Watch pines closely as they can experience a late burst of growth, and could suffer wire damage. If this occurs, remove the wire as soon as possible.

With the lower late autumn temperatures, the need to water is greatly reduced. Check the soil daily and water sparingly if required. Remember that strong wind can dry the soil very quickly. Give one or two applications of low or zero nitrogen fertilizer in early and mid-autumn to harden off the current year's growth. Fallen leaves should be removed from the soil surface and benches to minimize breeding places for

Right: In the summer months the trees will be growing steadily and will need to be trimmed regularly to keep them in shape. Remember to keep your bonsai trees well watered so that they are never allowed to dry out.

General Techniques 39

Above: Although they can be expensive, a high quality set of bonsai tools will simplify the task of trimming and pruning.

Left: Hardy trees may be left outside during the winter and generally only need protecting from the most extreme weather conditions. You will be able to see the shape and form of your trees clearly at this time of the year, and plan how you will shape them in the months ahead.

pests and diseases. Remove algae from trunks and branches by regularly brushing with a stiff brush and water.

Winter is a quiet time for your trees and you should leave all hardy trees outdoors throughout the season unless very extreme conditions occur when you may protect them until the most severe conditions have past. Now is a good time to study the form of all bonsai, particularly deciduous trees, to assess which branches, if any, will need pruning or adjusting to improve the shape of the tree.

Trees kept in the open will need little water, as they should receive enough from rain, mist and dew. Should they become too wet, place them under cover, but in the open, until they dry out a little. Your trees will not be harmed if their pots become covered in snow or even freeze for a short time. Clear away heavy snow from the branches, as the weight could damage them.

Get ready for spring by preparing your repotting soil during the winter. Mix and sift the soil, and make sure you have all the materials and tools ready when required.

Branch Pruning

Almost all bonsai will need to have one or more branches removed during their lives. This will normally be necessary to improve the appearance of a mature tree or to style the tree in the early stages of its training. The process of removing a branch is quite straightforward but care should always be taken to achieve the desired result. If carried out correctly, the wound should heal and leave little or no scar on the trunk or branch.

The cutters you use must be clean and sharp and it is sensible to cover the wound left by the pruning process with sealer that has been formulated specially for bonsai. If the wound is sealed correctly, the cut edge of the bark is prevented from drying out by the sealer and the healing process will be accelerated. If unwanted buds appear around the pruned area, pinch them off as soon as possible.

Pruning technique

Basic pruning can be done using a normal pair of secateurs but if you buy a good pair of bonsai branch pruners you will be able to carry out a much better and cleaner job of pruning. If you use the correct pair of cutters, you will be able to cut very close to the trunk and the wound will be concave in shape. Cut as close to the trunk as possible using the cutting edges at an angle of 90 degrees to the trunk. If you use the cutters with the edges vertical or parallel to the trunk, it is very likely that quite severe damage to the trunk will result.

If you use normal pruning secateurs, you will be left with a short stub that will not only look unsightly but also probably never heal over correctly. If you are left with a stub like this, it can be removed using a pair of knob cutters, which are concave in both directions of the

Right: This is the incorrect angle for using a branch cutter as it will cause damage to the trunk above and below the branch that is being removed.

General Techniques 41

cutting edges. This will leave a small concave hollow that will heal very much more quickly.

By leaving a hollow you will be aiding the callousing bark to 'roll' into the hollow and leave only a slight trace of the pruning exercise.

When pruning Japanese maples, never cut back shoots close to the next bud as the branch or shoot may die back beyond your chosen point. Always leave about 1.2cm (0.5in) of shoot to allow for dieback as this can be tidied up later.

Most techniques used for pruning branches are suitable for both conifers and deciduous trees but there are a few things to take into account when pruning branches from conifers. If you wish to remove a branch from a conifer, think carefully before taking off the whole branch. It may be that if you leave a short length of that branch in place, it could be stripped of its bark and used to create a feature called 'Jin' (see page 84). Jin is often seen on full-size conifers in the wild and particularly on pines and junipers.

Above left: This is the correct angle for the cutters to achieve a clean cut on the trunk.

Above: Using the more expensive knob cutters will give a similar result as the branch cutters, but they are less likely to damage the trunk because of the double curvature of their cutting edges.

Left: The reason for removing this branch is because mature trees, and well trained bonsai, do not generally have opposing branches at the same level on the trunk

Defoliating

As your bonsai trees develop, they will continue to produce a substantial amount of new growth each year. Throughout the growing period between April and early September, the rate of growth of some trees can be quite enormous so you will need to control their size and shape very closely. With deciduous trees this involves the need to pinch out the growing tips on a regular basis during the spring and summer.

Broadleaf trees generally produce shoots with pairs of leaves or single leaves on alternating sides of the shoot. These can be allowed to grow several pairs of leaves, and then each shoot is pinched back to one pair of leaves.

In some cases it is possible to remove all of the leaves on a deciduous tree, which is known as defoliating, so that the tree is deceived into thinking it is winter. This process is carried out only when the first set of leaves has matured, usually in late spring or very early summer and only then if the tree is in very good health. Of course, if you follow all the watering, feeding and general welfare techniques for bonsai your trees should all be healthy enough for defoliating to take place. A final comment on full defoliation – remember that this process should only be carried out once in two years on most trees. There are some trees that can be defoliated several times each year and these are the very vigorous growers, such as some of the maples.

The process of defoliation should result in the second crop of leaves being approximately two-thirds the size of the first set.

Conifers vary widely in the appearance of their tip growth, but the pruning technique for each is very similar.

Right: Acer palmatum *(Japanese maple) before carrying out the removal of any leaves.*

General Techniques 43

Above left: Remove leaves individually with sharp cutters, leaving the petiole (leaf stalk) to die back naturally.

Left: Continue to remove leaves from all over the tree.

Above: A partly defoliated tree showing the bare branches and removed leaves.

Below: Now you have a completely defoliated tree. This should be left in an open position and watered only when necessary.

Pine buds develop into 'candles'. When they are about 2.5cm (1in) long, pinch them back, using your fingers or a sharp pair of scissors, leaving about one third of their length.

Spruce and some junipers form small bunches of needles, which can be removed using your fingertips. Each week, remove the largest shoots, but make sure there is always some fresh growth remaining. If you remove all the green foliage from a conifer shoot the shoot will not survive.

Remember: you cannot completely defoliate evergreen conifers as they will not survive.

Experience is a very good teacher and as you become more familiar with your various trees then you will become aware of the best ways to deal with each type of plant.

Clip and Grow

The 'clip and grow' technique is one of the most straightforward styling actions in the world of bonsai. It is very simple in that it does not require you to undertake individual shoot pruning or pinching out which can be extremely time consuming.

This operation is derived from what is basically a Chinese technique that is closely allied to hedge trimming. You will probably already know that when you clip a hedge the surface of the hedge becomes twiggier and twiggier and the leaves gradually become smaller and smaller.

All you will need is a good pair of sharp scissors and the courage to set about your tree in an organized fashion. You simply clip the areas of foliage that need tidying up without worrying too much about cutting through leaves as you would in normal leaf or shoot pruning.

Starting from the lowest branch, clip the surface of the branch's foliage area until a neat and tidy appearance is achieved. Try to shape the foliage pad so that it looks natural and is wider nearer the trunk than the branch tip.

Repeat this process on the next branch up and continue like this until you reach the apex or canopy of the tree.

All of the trimmed branches should look similar in 'foliage weight' so the tree retains a balanced appearance.

As this operation is normally only applied to deciduous trees that will freely produce new leaves it can be carried out quite quickly, so it is

Below: This is a typical commercially available tree before any clipping has been carried out.

Below right: Using sharp cutters clip the various areas of foliage until they are neat and tidy.

Above: By clipping regularly you will start to create an attractive looking tree.

a very convenient way to deal with a lot of trees in a short time.

With the right type of material, such as Chinese elm or any other small leaf variety of tree, this can be a very successful way to develop the density of the branch twigs, which is also known as ramification. Each time the foliage areas on each branch are clipped, new buds will be stimulated to grow and within a few weeks the branch will again be fully foliated ready for the next clipping session.

This process can be carried out several times each season and as a result the twig density just gets better and better.

It does, however, eventually leave you with a tree that has dense pads on the branches. This seems to be a very Chinese style, which is excellent but not suitable for all types of tree. You may well find that to make a tree that has been trained by the 'clip and grow' method even better, you may wish to thin out the twigs so that the appearance does not look too dense.

46 The Beginner's Guide to Bonsai

Pruning for Shape

One of the main ways of shaping a bonsai is by pruning with scissors or branch cutters. This requires pruning in the correct place, in the correct way and at the correct time.

You may feel the need to purchase a good quality pair of bonsai scissors and possibly a similar quality pair of branch cutters although only scissors are used in this section. You may instead decide that you will be able to 'make do' with an ordinary pair of kitchen or general purpose scissors but they must have clean, sharp cutting edges.

After each pruning operation you can seal the wound with special bonsai wound seal or even a general-purpose sealer available from garden centres. In general this applies to larger cuts so if you are just trimming using scissors this will not normally be necessary.

In this section we are using a tree that has been trained as a bonsai for a number of years but which has been allowed to grow a little bit too much. The tree is in good condition but there are a lot of shoots that have grown out of all proportion to the trunk and branch structure.

Below: A 20-year-old Cercidiphyllum japonicum tree before reshaping.

Above: Prune the long shoots with sharp cutters near the base of each shoot leaving behind one pair of leaves.

Below: One half of the tree has been pruned and all the long shoots have been removed.

General Techniques 47

When trees have grown into a relatively mature shape, they will continue to produce a great amount of new growth every year. To maintain the mature shape, you need to pinch out the growing tips on a regular basis during the spring and summer. In this case neither of these operations was carried out and so it is now time to rectify the situation. Many people who grow bonsai find themselves in this sort of situation with trees that have been allowed to grow too much between prunings.

Using your scissors cut each extended shoot back to the outline of the original branch structure. Cut back so that only one or two leaves remain, or even further if you think it will benefit the overall shape of the tree. Continue removing shoots in this way until the whole tree has been tidied up so that it presents a good and balanced shape once again.

Deciduous trees tend to grow at quite alarming rates during the actual growing season, which can be four to five months long, and can easily get out of hand. Conifers are very much slower growers than deciduous trees and are, therefore, not so likely to be in need of such drastic pruning at any time of year.

Above: Continue to work around the tree, removing all of the long shoots with sharp cutters.

Far left: Keep checking the balance of the emerging tree – this picture shows that quite a lot of foliage may have to be removed to achieve the required result.

Left: The completed pruning reveals a mature-looking tree.

Wiring

Below: Push the end of the wire into the rootball to ensure that it is securely anchored.

Right: Coil the wire up the full length of the trunk at a 45 degree angle.

Far right: Bend the trunk carefully using both hands as support to prevent the trunk from cracking.

Wiring is certainly one of the most important and probably the most often used technique for bonsai training, as it enables you to position the trunk, branches and shoots accurately. This gives you control over the shape of the tree which, when complete, should look like a full-size mature tree but in miniature.

The wiring technique is straightforward, but requires persistence and practice to master. You should practise on branches of varying thickness to develop your skill before you begin on a serious bonsai project. You can practise on garden plants, for instance, where it does not matter so much if you break a branch or two. Get used to the feel of wire of different thicknesses and how easy or difficult it is to bend or manipulate them.

Annealed copper wire is traditionally used, but in recent years, anodized aluminium has become popular. It is easy to use and can be recycled without the use of heat treatment. Copper wire is still used but mainly by more experienced growers. Its special appeal is that it oxidizes very quickly and blends in with the bark colour.

The gauge, or thickness, of the wire used needs to be thick enough to hold the branch in place after bending. If you use a wire that is too thin to work properly you will have to remove it and start over again using a thicker gauge.

Check the flexibility of branches before applying wire, as some species are more brittle than others.

You will find that maples can be very brittle and care should be taken when bending these branches. However, if you are using a juniper or pine you will find the branches are very much more flexible and amenable to manipulation.

Young branches are normally more flexible than more mature ones. Very old branches, of course, can be very thick and stubborn and so will need other techniques applied, but beginners do not normally carry out these procedures on old stock.

General Techniques 49

Far left: The reshaped trunk now reveals a more interesting shape.

Left: Anchor a piece of wire to the trunk by making two turns in the middle around the trunk. Then take each end out onto two separate branches and coil these along each branch.

Above left: Continue to coil the wire right to the tips of each branch.

Above: This pine tree has been wired and the branches have been bent to create interesting shapes.

The correct type of cutters will be an asset, as they will enable you to cut the wire close to the tree, without damaging the bark.

The best way to start is to do a trial run on a flexible piece of branch that is not too critical if things should go wrong. Use a length of wire about half the thickness of the branch. Hold the wire to the branch with one hand, and wind it around and along the branch with the other. The wire should lie neatly on the trunk or branch, run at an angle of about 45 degrees, and should not be too tight or too loose. Your piece of wire will need to be about one and a half times the length of the branch or branches that you are going to deal with. Remember to allow a sufficient length of wire so that you can get a good grip on the wire at each end.

Check the wired branch regularly to see if the wire is cutting into the branch. In fact, the wire does not cut into the branch, rather the bark grows up and around the wire and will eventually give the appearance of 'cutting in'. When you see signs of this happening, remove the wire immediately. If the branch stays in place when the wire is removed then you need do nothing else at that moment. If, however, the branch does not remain where you want it to be, then you must be prepared to rewire the branch again.

Root Pruning

The most important aspect of bonsai is understanding and maintaining a young and healthy root structure as the roots are responsible for providing the trees with water and nutrients without which they will not survive.

Regular root pruning and soil renewal will generate a young root system, disease free and clear of unwanted infestations. Age and the species of the tree will dictate the frequency of this operation. The active root system will always be the youngest part of the tree. Root pruning and repotting should be carried out in early spring, just before buds begin to break. It is better to root prune in the spring so that new roots begin to start growing immediately. Root pruning encourages many young feeder roots to develop, which will lead to healthy growth in the upper part of the tree.

The first step is to remove the tree carefully from its existing pot. Using a rake or chopstick, untangle and comb the roots to remove the soil from the outside of the root ball so that the roots all hang down freely. A single root hook is ideal for untangling the thicker, more complicated roots. Using sharp scissors, trim the roots on all sides as well as from the underside so that the roots appear as a circular, flat pad. A neat and tidy appearance should be the aim whilst leaving sufficient fibrous roots in place to support the tree when it is repotted.

Left: Carefully remove the tree and its root ball from its original pot.

Above: Using a special bonsai rake, or a bent fork, loosen the soil so that the roots hang free.

General Techniques

Far left: Rake around the complete root structure untangling all roots to facilitate pruning

Left: Remove excess roots using sharp cutters.

Below left: Remove any large roots using a branch or knob cutter. This will encourage a finer and more shallow root structure to develop.

Below: Prune back excess branch growth to cut down on transpiration and to assist the redevelopment of the root structure.

Repotting

Prepare the chosen pot as described in the relevant section of this book and add a layer of coarse grit or Akadama to the bottom of the pot. Position the tree so that it is slightly behind and to one side of the pot's centre lines. This positioning is appropriate when using rectangular or oval pots but when using a round, square, multisided or regular shaped pot, the tree should normally be placed in the centre. A useful tip when potting is to place a small mound of soil under the tree's root ball.

Twist the tree clockwise and anti-clockwise while pushing the tree down into the pot. This will ensure that the roots make good contact with the soil.

Bring the two ends of the tying-in wire together over the root ball and, using a pair of pliers, twist the two ends, pulling at the same time, until the tree if firmly fixed into the pot.

Add soil until the pot is full and then work the soil in around the roots with a chopstick or something similar. It is always better to use dry soil as this allows it to be worked into the root ball correctly. Carefully brush off any excess soil and water thoroughly.

Balancing root and top growth

If major pruning of roots and top growth is to be carried out at the same time, consideration should be given to achieving a balanced approach to the exercise. In other words, if you need to cut away half of the roots, you may need to remove half of the foliage at the same time. This allows the tree to balance its root and top growth activity.

Following repotting, the soil should be kept just moist so that the tree is able to support new roots without any fear of waterlogging.

Below: Add a shallow base layer of soil across the bottom of a pot that has been prepared with wire to hold the tree in place (see pages 32-33).

Below right: Secure the tree in the pot by bringing the two ends of the wire together and twisting to tighten them.

General Techniques 53

Far left: Top up the soil to within about 1cm (0.4in) of the rim of the pot.

Left: Work soil into and around the roots of the tree using a chopstick.

Below: Water the repotted bonsai gently to avoid disturbing the soil.

Below left: The soil colour has now darkened indicating that it has absorbed the water completely.

Below: After a few weeks the repotted bonsai is growing well and showing its fresh spring colours.

Watering

Water is just as important to a bonsai as it is to a human – without it, neither can survive. If a human is thirsty, it will take a drink. If a bonsai is thirsty, it also needs to drink, and it is up to the human bonsai grower to make sure that sufficient water is available.

If your trees are kept outside, they may receive natural rainfall but you should not be fooled into thinking that they will get enough water from this source. Some trees have a very dense foliage canopy and even with heavy rainfall the water can be shed from the foliage and over the edge of the pot, just as we would use an umbrella to protect ourselves from rain. On such occasions, you will need to supplement the natural watering by adding water to the soil of your bonsai yourself. You can do this by using a watering can fitted with a fine rose or, if you have a very large collection of trees, use a hose, which should also have a fine rose attached.

The need to water will depend on many factors. Strong sun or wind, or a combination of both, can soon lead to a drought situation in the bonsai pot, so you should check the moisture level in the soil regularly.

The watering techniques described above apply to outdoor trees. Slightly different techniques apply to indoor trees. It is very easy to water them by just submerging the whole pot in a bowl of water, completely covering the soil with water. Bubbles will begin to rise from the soil, wait until they stop rising, remove your bonsai from the water and allow it to drain.

Indoor trees can also be watered using a watering can. Direct the water onto the soil surface using a general purpose can with or without a rose attached. Be careful you do not wash away any of the soil during this process.

Indoor trees may need some extra humidity around their foliage. To increase the humidity

Right: With a large collection of bonsai the easiest way to water is by using a hose with a multipurpose spray gun attached, making sure that the soil is well watered. Even after heavy rainfall the soil may not have absorbed water if the foliage on the tree is very dense.

General Techniques

Above left: Misting. You should mist the foliage of indoor bonsai regularly using a commercially available mist sprayer.

Above: Small trees can be watered using a small watering can.

Above: Dunking. Place the bonsai in a bowl of water completely submerging the pot and soil.

Above right: Leave the pot and tree submerged until no more air bubbles rise from the soil.

Right: Spraying. Spray the leaves of outdoor bonsai occasionally in the evenings during prolonged spells of very hot weather.

around the foliage of a bonsai, you can place a layer of absorbent granules or grit into the bottom of a shallow dish or tray. Keep the granules or grit moist at all times, so that when you place your indoor bonsai onto the grit in the tray, the evaporating water from the tray drifts up and around the foliage. This will slow down the rate of transpiration of water from the leaves and reduce the risk of them drying out.

Feeding

Feeding at the correct time of year with the right type of fertilizer is just as important as watering. If good healthy growth is to be maintained, a good feeding regime is essential. Fertilizers can be added during the watering process but a certain amount of the applied fertilizer will be washed out of the soil, which means that nutrients will need to be added at regular intervals throughout the growing season.

Fertilizers are available in a variety of forms, liquid, soluble powder, slow release granules, and pellets. These can be applied by spraying onto the foliage, watering onto the soil or by placing pellets onto the soil surface.

Liquid and soluble powder fertilizers should be mixed with water, in the proportions recommended on the container, and applied to the soil using a watering can with a rose attached. Fertilizer pellets are usually available from specialist bonsai suppliers and they are normally rape seed cake. This is a slow release fertilizer and will supply the feeding requirements of your bonsai for several weeks before the need to add more. These need to be placed on the soil surface arranging them at about 5cm (2in) intervals around, and just in from, the edge of the pot. If you wish, you can make small holes with a chopstick and push the pellets into the holes, covering them over with a small amount of soil.

Foliar feeding

Foliar feeding can be carried out using a liquid foliar feed and applying it with an atomizing sprayer. Keep to the recommended dose as spraying with a more concentrated feed may well cause leaf damage.

Bio Gold rape cake fertilizer

Osmocote slow release fertilizer

Q4 fertilizer

Above: Position fertilizer pellets at regular intervals around the pot. Place them on, or just below, the surface of the soil.

Frequent applications of half-strength liquid or soluble fertilizer, approximately once a week, is the easiest course of action, and slow release pellets should be applied about twice during the growing season. Some slow release fertilizers are made in the form of a soil additive and they can be mixed with the soil at repotting time. This will give a balanced background feed through the season but may need to be supplemented by applying liquid or solid feed.

Feeding should take place from spring to late summer, with an autumn feed of low or zero nitrogen content to harden off the current year's growth, which will help the tree to survive through the winter.

Most fertilizers contain nitrogen (N), phosphorus (P) and potassium (K). This is usually quoted on the package as an NPK ratio, such as NPK 6:12:10.

Leaf and stem growth requires nitrogen, which is responsible for the rich green colours of the leaves. Too much nitrogen will force the trees to grow at an excessive rate and make it more difficult to control their growth. It is best to use a balanced fertilizer with a fairly low nitrogen content to achieve steady growth.

Phosphorus is responsible for healthy root growth, helping the trees' bud formation and protection against diseases and adverse winter conditions. Potassium (potash) helps with the formation of flowers and fruit, protection against disease and hardens off growth before the winter.

Most commercially available fertilizers contain all three main nutrients plus some trace elements, which provide the trees with all the other minor essential ingredients that are needed for healthy growth.

An early autumn low or zero nitrogen feed will help your trees through the winter. You can use a fertilizer such as tomato feed or a special zero nitrogen feed, known as 0-10-10 in the bonsai world for this application.

Regular Maintenance

If you are planning to exhibit your bonsai, you will need to take care that the tree and pot are both clean and tidy. There are a few procedures that should be closely followed which will help you to achieve this. Your trees and pots should always be clean and tidy, as this will deter unwanted pests and diseases. Remember that when showing trees at exhibitions they must be at their very best.

Remove damaged leaves with your fingers, or tweezers if they are difficult to reach, and eliminate dieback within the branch structure using scissors for small items or branch cutters for the larger ones. Brushing with a stiff brush and water will remove algae and moss from the trunk and branches. Spraying with water whilst brushing will wash away any dislodged debris. Loose pieces of bark should be carefully removed with tweezers taking care not to damage any natural elements that may enhance the final appearance of the tree. Any signs of disease or insect attack should also be removed and the tree treated to stop any recurrence of the problem.

The appearance of the soil surface and the cleanliness of the pots are also very important aspects of general maintenance and when preparing bonsai for exhibition. Dead leaves or needles should be removed from the surface of the soil, along with any other unsightly bits and pieces, such as weeds and loose moss. This can be achieved by brushing the soil surface with a suitable brush and picking out individual unwanted small plants (weeds) with a pair of tweezers. Liverwort and pearlwort are two of the most troublesome unwanted plants that may be found growing on the top of the soil and they can be removed using tweezers. Liverwort is a sign that the soil is generally too wet and pearlwort can choke the tree roots. Pearlwort roots go deep into and under the root ball and often block the drainage holes. This makes the soil too wet that in turn may lead to the development and spread of liverwort.

Pots should be brushed and washed clean and allowed to dry. A standard kitchen scouring pad is ideal for scrubbing dirty pots to remove algae,

Below: Clean a dirty pot by rubbing it vigorously with a scouring pad, stiff brush or any other implement that will remove unwanted particles and algae.

Below right: The cleaned pot now looks ready for entering an exhibition.

calcium deposits and any other general deposits that create a dirty appearance. You may enhance the look and colour of a pot with a light spray of 'leaf shine' or something similar, such as a light wipe over with vegetable oil using a lint-free cloth. I prefer to use 'leaf shine' as it dries off quickly and gives the pot a very natural appearance and resists the reappearance of all of the troublesome elements that have been cleaned away previously.

Left: Carefully remove unwanted weeds and moss from around the base of the tree using tweezers.

Left: Brush the trunk base briskly to remove moss so that the surface roots can be clearly seen.

Below left: The surface roots are now clean and the interesting root formation can be clearly seen.

Below: Finally, remove any tiny pieces of moss and loose particles with with a coco brush.

Pests and Diseases

Bonsai are just as susceptible to pests and diseases as full-size trees. To prevent problems relating to these, apply a systemic insecticide or fungicide about twice a year. These are available as soil or foliage products and are absorbed by the plant to give protection for several months. Apply a 'winter wash' to eliminate overwintering eggs and grubs hidden in cracks on the trunk and branches. You can purchase these products from your garden accessories supplier but do be aware that it is becoming increasingly difficult to find effective products. This is because there is ever more legislation that restricts the sale of pesticides and insecticides because of their possible danger to human health.

There are a number of pests that can be a particular problem to bonsai trees. The vine weevil grub can quickly kill a tree. It feeds on the roots destroying the tree's lifeline. The grub strips the roots up to soil level only so that it is not obvious there is a problem until the tree begins to wilt and die. Treat the soil at regular intervals with a suitable product to prevent infestation and repot with fresh soil at the correct time of year. If you find grubs when repotting, wash the roots clean of all soil and repot in the usual way.

The adult vine weevil hides away during the day emerging at night to eat notches from leaf edges. Treat with insecticide or go out after dark with a torch and collect adults from leaves and destroy them.

Scale insects can be difficult to detect until the limpet-like shell lifts, and a sticky white mass appears from beneath. Applying systemic insecticide can prevent this or you can physically remove the adult scale one by one. A cotton bud soaked in methylated spirit can be effective in the removal of scale from the trunks of bonsai. Alternatively you can take them off with a stiff brush, such as an old toothbrush, but unfortunately this may just transfer them down to the soil from where they could reappear later.

Aphids can also be a problem and they take many forms, such as greenfly, blackly and whitefly. The most troublesome pests on indoor bonsai are whitefly and scale, and regular applications of some form of insecticide will control them.

Woolly aphid is a particular problem on pines, larch and beech and appears as a white, fluffy, sticky mass. On pines and larch it occurs among the needles and on beech on the underside of the leaves. Once again treating with systemic insecticide should do the trick.

Diseases on bonsai are not as frequently encountered as pests and generally take the form of leaf disorders which can normally be kept under control by removing and destroying affected leaves.

Good hygienic practices will normally keep most pests and diseases under control. This should reduce the need to use insecticides and pesticides, so use these sparingly and carefully only if other removal methods fail.

Below: Vine weevils are seldom seen as they feed at night, eating notches from the edges of foliage. They are not generally a problem unless allowed to lay their eggs in the soil which results in larvae.

General Techniques

Above left: Scale insects suck the sap from plants and slowly kill them. A secondary infestation of sooty mould is usually an indication that these pests are present. You can kill scale insects by using a systemic insecticide.

Above: Blackfly are serious leaf pests, usually in early spring, when they appear suddenly in large clusters on young shoots, sucking the sap and deforming the foliage. Treat with systemic insecticide to destroy them.

Left: Vine weevil larvae are one of the most destructive potted plant pests. They rapidly eat plant roots so that the foliage wilts suddenly and the plant usually dies. Treat affected plants with commercially available insecticides.

Below: Pine rust affects two-needle pines such as Scots pine. Spores infect the tree's needles and developing shoots in summer, causing them to turn brown and die. Treat affected plants with a proprietary brand fungicide.

Left: Green aphids are similar to blackfly in appearance. There are many different variations of aphids, and they all cause similar damage to foliage. They can be dealt with by using a systemic insecticide.

Chapter 4

Creating a Bonsai

A bonsai can be made from almost any type of plant material that will eventually produce a good mature woody trunk, which resembles one that you would find on a full-size tree.

Begin by going to a reputable plant supplier and choose a plant that may have the potential for making a bonsai. You will need to look at the base of the trunk to see if there is the possibility of a good root and trunk buttress. Have a close look and scrape away some of the soil surface to find where the roots begin to emerge from the trunk. Look at the branch structure to see if it has a good balanced set of branches, preferably with thick low branches and thinner upper branches.

Using the techniques described in previous sections of this book, you should be able to create some reasonable starter trees from which your collection will inevitably grow.

The techniques employed to create your bonsai trees will encompass the whole range from root pruning through branch pruning to wiring and watering, in fact whatever is needed to obtain a good result.

European Olive

The European olive, or *Olea europaea* to give it its botanical name, is also known as the common olive or edible olive and is usually found growing wild in Mediterranean countries where it is also grown on farms for its fruit. It has approximately 8cm (3in) long, lanceolate, grey-green leaves while the underside is a slightly fluffy silver-green. Its flowers are off-white and fragrant and its fruit is green, which ripens to red and purplish-black olives up to 4cm (1.5in) long.

This is the plant whose fruit is the olive that is well known for its culinary uses. It is readily available in most modern garden centres as they are sold for use as houseplants as well as conservatory plants or even as garden plants in certain milder frost-free areas. It can withstand quite low temperatures for short periods but should never be exposed to temperatures below about -5°C (23°F).

The plant used here for making into a bonsai started at about 35cm (14in) tall and during the styling process it was reduced to approximately 25cm (10in). The roots were raked, untangled and pruned with scissors and knob cutters so that it could be finally potted into a 13cm (5in) square bonsai pot. The angle at which it was placed into the pot was determined so that the relatively simple branch structure could easily be seen when viewed from the front. In this way it begins to have the look of a tree in its overall appearance. This is a very straightforward piece of material, which resulted in a very simple design. As such it would be highly suitable as an experimental tree for beginners who are learning the art of bonsai.

The so-called 'finished' tree will take several years to reach its full potential by which time it will probably have been allowed to grow to about 28cm (11in) in height and realize a width of roughly the same dimension. It will need to have its shoots regularly pinched out at the tips to encourage more bushy growth after which some thinning of branches may be necessary to achieve the best end result. This, then, is the early stage of a simple indoor bonsai.

Below: The simple, inexpensive Olea europea *(European olive) shown as it is available from most plant centres before any bonsai work has been carried out.*

Below right: Begin by removing excess long growth using sharp cutters.

Creating a Bonsai 65

Left: By carefully removing excess growth, the beginnings of a bonsai can be clearly seen.

Above: Any ugly stubs from previous pruning should be removed cleanly using a knob cutter.

Above: After careful pruning has been completed, the tree is ready for potting.

Right: The finished olive tree has now been planted in a square glazed pot – the first step to becoming a successful bonsai specimen.

Bigleaf Podocarp

Below: When buying from a garden centre, try to choose a plant that has an interesting shape with branches that offer potential for the bonsai that you hope to create.

Below right: The longest branches have been removed using sharp cutters to form a more compact shape for the emerging tree.

The *Podocarpus macrophyllus* is often referred to as Kusumaki or bigleaf podocarp and is native to Southern China. Some varieties are used for timber production.

It can make a shrub up to 2m (6.5ft) in height or a tree up to about 15m (50ft) depending on its natural habitat. As with most trees or shrubs, it will respond to techniques used in bonsai culture. It has leaves that are approximately 8-11cm (3-4in) long that are linear lanceolate or 'long and narrow'. They are dark green above and yellow-green below. It also has catkin like cones that are about 35cm (14in) long.

This variety is hardy down to about -25°C (-13°F) but it is usually sold as an indoor bonsai in temperate areas where it is also almost always hardy as an outdoor bonsai. It is quite easy to propagate from cuttings but remember that cuttings from an erect part of the plant tend to give upright trees and from side shoots you will get prostrate plants. *Podocarpus* is generally free from pests and diseases so it could make an ideal starter plant for bonsai.

To create this *Podocarpus* bonsai the plant chosen was about 50cm (20in) tall, including the pot. Through the basic bonsai styling processes this was reduced to about 25cm (10in). As this is a fairly unusual shape the chosen 'front', or best viewing side, seemed to be where you would be able to enjoy the best view of the branching structure. The roots were raked out and pruned, making sure that the balance between the roots and the top growth was in proportion as described in an earlier section. The tree was eventually planted into a 23 x 17cm (9 x 6.5in) rectangular bonsai pot.

Creating a Bonsai 67

Far left: Now you can start carefully to remove branches and foliage using sharp cutters. Do not try to rush this stage of pruning as it is easy to get carried away and spoil your tree.

Left: Continue to remove branches, turning the plant as you work to check that the overall effect is well balanced. Try to keep in mind the shape of the finished bonsai that you are hoping to create.

As with all plants in their early years as bonsai, this tree will require several years to reach full maturity by when it will have grown to between 30 to 35cm (12 to 14in) in height and in width. Again, this tree will require its shoot tips to be regularly pinched out to encourage a bushier growth pattern. As time goes on, you will need to monitor the tree's growth and thin out as and when necessary to achieve the required balance within the structure of the tree. Some thinning of branches may be necessary over the next few years to achieve the interesting tree-like form upon which all bonsai depend.

Above left: Finally, ensure that you have removed all of the unwanted branches to complete the bonsai shaping process.

Above: The completed tree has now been potted into a rectangular container and already looks like a convincing bonsai.

Japanese Maple

Below: This pot grown Acer may not look very much like a bonsai at the moment, but with some careful thought and a little work it will be transformed into a stunning specimen.

Below right: The tree has been removed from its pot, exposing previously unseen areas of trunk and has been tilted at a more interesting angle. It is standing on a turntable that makes it easy to rotate the tree when working on it.

The *Acer palmatum* is commonly referred to as the Japanese maple and there are hundreds of varieties and cultivars. It is native to Japan and Korea and has become one of the most popular decorative small trees throughout the world. In the wild it can grow to 8m (26ft) in height and will have an apex that is rounded. The *dissectum* will have five to nine lobed leaves incised almost to their base and the lobes are generally serrated to some degree. The leaves can be anything up to 10cm (4in) long but that will reduce considerably when the pruning practices used for bonsai are employed.

The Japanese maple is one of the most popular trees from which bonsai can be made as they react well to all the usual bonsai techniques. It is one of those plants that can produce quite long internodal growth and, as such, will need close monitoring during the growing season, from April to September, with regular shoot tip pinching being required.

All Japanese maples are hardy down to very low minus centigrade temperatures and will always be sold as hardy outdoor plants in temperate climates. That makes them highly suitable for use as outdoor bonsai as they will withstand practically any sort of weather conditions that occur in temperate climates. Almost all cultivars are propagated by grafting and there is a very large selection of varieties available from plant suppliers that can be grown as bonsai. The colour and leaf shape variation of the different cultivars is enormous, so there should be a variety available suitable for anyone who is thinking of making a colourful, relatively easy-to-maintain bonsai.

Choosing a plant

The plant chosen to start this bonsai was 45cm (18in) high, including the pot, and 45cm (18in) across. Once again using normal bonsai styling techniques it was reduced slightly to about 25cm

Creating a Bonsai 69

Far left: Remove some of the branches to be able to see the true form of the tree. As more branches are removed, the improving shape is revealed.

Left: By applying wire to some of the branches, the shape can be improved by carefully bending them.

Far left: The wiring is complete and the branches can be repositioned to create more interesting shapes.

Left: The completed tree is planted at an angle in a suitable round pot.

Below: All of the leaves are carefully removed to allow the tree to concentrate on forming new roots.

(10in) in height. Following the initial styling, the root ball was checked, raked out as in the repotting section, pruned and the most interesting side of the tree chosen as the front, or best viewing side. It was potted into a very good quality 24cm (9.5in) diameter container. The pot may not be the ideal final container for the tree but at this stage it appears to be highly suitable because of its glazed finish, colour and shape which complement the plant admirably.

This plant – as with all other bonsai in training – will require several years before full maturity is reached and it will finally be around 30cm (12in) in overall height and width. The tree's growth will need to be checked regularly with leaves, shoots and branches being pruned when required, so maintaining the balance between the trunk and branch structure.

Weeping Fig

Above: This bushy weeping fig is typical of the plant variety that can be found in most garden centres, nurseries and supermarkets. It is ideal for turning into a bonsai and a good choice for the beginner.

Weeping fig, Benjamin tree, tropical laurel and the small leaved rubber plant are some of the more commonly used names for the *Ficus benjamina* in various parts of the world. Material of this plant variety is very freely available as houseplants and may be obtained from almost any garden centre, nursery or supermarket. Many tropical or sub-tropical plants that are used as houseplants can often be turned into a bonsai and the weeping fig is probably one of the most straightforward to use. The variety used here is called 'Bushy King' and its compact form makes it an ideal choice for someone starting out in bonsai.

These plants originate from a wide area including south and south-east Asia through to northern Australia and the south-west Pacific. They normally require a fairly humid atmosphere with temperatures ranging from 10 to 18°C (50 to 64°F) and they can be kept indoors or in a greenhouse or conservatory in temperate areas of the world.

This variety has a wealth of variegated leaves as its dominant feature, but you always need to look at the trunk formation to see if it would look good when transformed into the tree-like form required for bonsai. Here you will have to use your imagination to decide if your chosen plant will be suitable as a bonsai. This type of plant can have one or more trunks and quite often will have a very interesting root system.

The *Ficus benjamina* used here was about 60cm (24in) tall, including the pot, before any work was carried out. After the styling and potting exercise had been finished, the overall height was 38cm (15in). It is obvious that a large amount of top growth needed to be removed as well as a substantial amount of roots. However, in the case of the roots, not such a large proportion of the overall plant volume was removed.

The plant – which will become a bonsai after styling – first needed to have a few lower branches removed so that the base of the trunk could be seen. It was then easier to see which was the best viewing side and from then on it was more obvious how much pruning had to be carried out to achieve a good end result. The normal procedures for root preparation were used as described on previous pages with the tree eventually being potted into an 18 x 15cm (7 x 6in) rectangular glazed green pot, which appears to suit it very well.

Right: The plant has been removed from its pot and placed on a turntable which allows for easy rotation of the tree during styling.

Far right: The small lower shoots have been removed to expose the trunk.

Creating a Bonsai 71

Above: The long shoots of growth – at the right-hand top of the plant – have been removed and the new form of the tree is starting to emerge.

Right: Continue to shape the plant by removing the central top growth.

Regular misting of the foliage with water is beneficial and the soil should be kept just moist at all times. Feed lightly, but regularly, during the main growing season from spring to autumn.

As new shoots grow, prune them back leaving just one or two leaves. Caution should be applied when pruning *Ficus*, as at every cut, however small, the plant will secrete a sticky white fluid called latex which is very toxic. It should be thoroughly washed from hands and never allowed to get near to the eyes or mouth.

Above left: The remaining long shoots on the left side have been removed and the pruning is now complete.

Above: The finished tree has now been potted into a green glazed rectangular pot which complements the colour of the plant's foliage. Always consider the angle at which you will pot your tree trunk as this will affect the visual balance.

Chapter 5
Advanced Techniques

This chapter covers a few techniques that are a little more advanced than would normally be expected of a beginner to bonsai such as layering, grafting, rock planting, jin, sharamiki and forest plantings. There are many more to discover but these are just tasters to whet your appetite and to take you a little way beyond the most basic bonsai techniques.

Also in this section we will consider collecting a plant or tree from a garden or from the wild. This technique is used to acquire a piece of material that already has an aged thick trunk that will give a bonsai enthusiast a head start towards creating a good quality tree.

Layering

The most common layering techniques are ground and air layering. Ground layering is not often used in bonsai work but air layering is a common practice employed to create roots where they are best suited for bonsai production. Here we are air layering on a plant to produce roots at a point on the existing trunk where they would better suit the relationship of the trunk and root ball. It is a simple technique and can be easily mastered.

Layering is a vegetative method of propagation by which a shoot or stem of a plant is encouraged to produce roots. Some plants will layer naturally when their branches droop and make contact with the ground. Most woody plants can be layered and where it is difficult to propagate from seeds or cuttings, it may still be possible by layering. This is a good technique for producing plants for bonsai purposes.

Air layering is commonly used to produce roots at any point above soil level on woody plants. For bonsai this technique is mostly used to produce an annular root system around the trunk above soil level.

Using a sharp knife make two cuts, 2.5cm (1in) apart, around the trunk and into the bark to the heartwood. Make one cut between and at right angles to the original cuts also through to the heartwood. Using the knife tip, prise the bark away as a complete band exposing the heartwood beneath. Wrap about two handfuls of wet sphagnum moss around the exposed area taking it well above and below the cut lines. Root production may be improved by dusting the exposed ends of the bark or cambium layer with hormone rooting powder.

Right: This Zelkova serrata stock plant was selected for its interesting zig-zag trunk. Make two cuts around the bark about 2.5cm (1in) apart using a sharp knife.

Right: Using the tip of the knife prise the bark away from the heartwood. Continue carefully so that the strip of bark comes away cleanly in one piece.

Far right: The strip of bark has been completely removed exposing the heartwood of the tree.

Advanced Techniques 75

Far left: Freshly collected sphagnum moss soaked in water.

Left: Wrap about two handfuls of wet sphagnum moss around the ring-barked area of the trunk and press it firmly into place.

Left: Wrap a piece of black polythene around the sphagnum to help it retain its moisture.

Above: Tie around the black polythene at the top and bottom using wire or string to make an airtight seal.

Cover the moss with a strip of black polythene, tying close to the trunk with string or wire. Make sure that the ties are airtight so reducing moisture loss from the layered area. This can be carried out from early spring to mid-summer but make sure that time is allowed for good root development by the end of the summer. This is when the newly rooted plant can be cut from the parent. In late summer remove the polythene and gently expose the area of removed bark. Carefully cut off just below the new root system. At this stage, the roots are very fragile so take care when potting into its new container. Use a good open soil mixture when potting and protect the delicate roots from frost over the first winter.

Left: The completed air layering. In late summer remove the polythene and a new root system should have formed in the ball of sphagnum moss. Carefully cut off the trunk just below the new root system and pot in a new container, taking care not to damage the fragile roots.

Grafting

Grafting can be used to add a branch or trunk to an existing tree to improve its form and make it a better bonsai. Root grafting, inarch grafting and thread grafting are three of the most commonly used methods during bonsai training. All of them may seem daunting to the beginner at first but you will soon see that it is not as difficult as you may have imagined. To improve the appearance of a bonsai, a new branch can be added and thread grafting is frequently the best course of action to achieve this.

Like full-size trees, bonsai can naturally shed branches and by grafting a new branch onto the area from where the tree has shed its old branch, we can rectify this situation.

Thread grafting is used to add such a branch to a tree in a way that will improve its overall appearance. This is a very simple operation consisting of initially growing a long shoot on the tree, which can then be threaded through a drilled hole in the trunk and left to graft naturally into the trunk.

Drilling and wiring

The shoot may need to be grown for one or two seasons so that it is long enough for the purpose before stripping it of all its foliage and side shoots. This technique cannot be carried out on a conifer because stripping a shoot of its foliage will result in the death of that shoot. Drill a hole through the selected part of the trunk large enough to accommodate the new branch. Apply wire to about half of the branch to act as support, and carefully bend the branch around before threading the end through the drilled hole. Push the new branch as far as it will go into the hole, passing the wire around the back of the trunk and onto the branch end to secure it on the exit side. Seal the new branch on both sides of the trunk and leave for at least one growing season before cutting it off at the entrance point on the trunk. By this time the new branch should have grafted satisfactorily onto the trunk.

Right: A tree has been selected from nursery stock with suitably long branches for thread grafting.

Right: Remove the larger side branch leaving just a single branch.

Far right: Remove all of the remaining leaves and side shoots from the selected branch.

Advanced Techniques

Far left: All of the leaves and side shoots have been stripped from the branch and it is now ready for wiring.

Left: Half of the branch has now been wired along the area of maximum curvature to prevent it snapping while bending it into place.

Far left: Now drill a hole through the the trunk large enough to accept the new branch to be grafted into place. The hole should be drilled at an angle that will match the position of the finally grafted branch.

Left: Drill right through the trunk prior to the insertion of the new branch.

Above: The stripped branch is threaded into the drilled hole in the trunk and pulled cleanly through. Coil the remaining wire around to the end of the branch to secure it in its new position.

Right: Seal the joints at both sides of the trunk using special horticultural sealant that is available from bonsai nurseries and larger garden centres for this purpose.

Planting a Forest or Group

A forest or group is normally made up of anything from five trees to as many as you think you can handle. The number of trees included should always be an odd number as this tends to give a more balanced appearance.

Producing a good forest planting may take some time and several experimental plantings before you achieve a natural looking arrangement. You should try to recreate a group that gives you the feeling of being in the forest that you have planted, while still remembering that you and others will be viewing it from the outside.

There are many types of trees that are suitable for creating a forest or group, but keeping to the same species and variety for individual forests generally gives a better overall appearance. In the wild, you can find small groups of trees made up of mixed species, so why not try this also, as it could be very successful.

In the final arrangement it is important that the group should give the impression of depth, perspective and reality. The group should not include any three trees in a straight line and no trunk should be completely hidden one behind another, when viewed from the front or side. Containers for this style are ideally shallow ovals or rectangles while a thin slab of slate or rock would make an excellent alternative. It is also possible to make your own slabs from reinforced fibreglass or concrete, both of which can be coloured to simulate natural rock. The pot should be prepared in advance as described in the section dealing with pot preparation. You may need to include plenty of wires for securing the trees to the pot.

Choose several trees of the same variety making sure that you have one tree that is larger than the rest. A group planting always needs to have one tree that dominates the remainder to act as a focal point. The lower branches will need to be removed from the main tree before positioning into the prepared pot, just right of centre and about halfway back.

The second largest tree can then be placed close to the main tree. Some of the branches may

Below: This forest clump of Acer buergerianum *shows how impressive a carefully planned group planting can appear.*

Below right: A group of Acer palmatum 'Shindeshojo' *plants have been carefully selected and are ready for assembling into a forest.*

Advanced Techniques 79

Left: Remove the trees from their pots, rake away any excess soil and trim the roots so that they will fit closely together in their new container.

Above: Select a suitable flat pot – a large drainage hole is essential.

Above: Cut enough pieces of plastic mesh to cover each drainage hole.

Right: Secure the mesh over each hole as described on pages 32-33.

need to be removed from any of the trees that are to be part of the inner section of the group, so that they can sit close together, but not become confused with each other.

After trimming branches and roots to suit, position the rest of the trees one at a time close to each other so that they begin to form a natural looking arrangement. The smaller trees will need to be placed on the outside of the group so that all of the trees look as if they have been growing in those positions for many years. Making sure that the trees are secure and firm in the pot, top up the soil by working it in and around the roots with a chopstick as described previously and water well to settle the trees into the pot.

Trim any remaining long shoots to give a tidy and balanced overall appearance and place outdoors in a shady spot to acclimatise.

Above: Sprinkle a base layer of soil over the bottom of the pot.

80 The Beginner's Guide to Bonsai

Above: Position the main (tallest) tree slightly to one side of centre in the pot.

Above right: Position the second tree (multi-trunk) close to the first.

Right: There are now three trees in place.

Far right: The fourth tree is placed behind the first three giving more perspective to the arrangement.

Far left: The fifth tree is positioned alongside the others in the group.

Left: All of the trees are now in position which completes the arrangement of the group. Already it looks like a miniature forest.

Advanced Techniques

Left: Top up the soil around the root balls and trunks of the newly-planted trees.

Above: Work the soil in and around the roots of the trees using a chopstick.

Right: The completed group after watering showing the capillary adhesion of Akadama granules and the draining of excess water from the pot.

Above: The completed forest group after any excess soil has been brushed away. Now the plants are ready for watering.

Right: Six weeks later, the group is now starting to become well established, creating a most attractive bonsai forest.

Rock Planting

Planting trees with the root system established over, on or in a rock can give a very natural and inspirational appearance. There are many places in the countryside where trees growing naturally in such conditions can be seen.

There are several types of rock plantings commonly used in bonsai growing. These are: Root in Rock, Root on Rock and Root over Rock and their names accurately describe the positioning of the roots relative to the piece of rock.

The Root on Rock style depends upon being able to find a suitable piece of plant material and a matching piece of rock so that the roots can be attached to the surface of the rock. With this style the roots on the rock will mostly be covered with soil and moss and will not necessarily extend down to soil level. With Root over Rock the roots of the tree will cascade, exposed, over the rock with the active roots buried in the soil beneath the rock. Finally, the Root in Rock style will have the roots growing in a natural or man-made crevice in the piece of rock which will contain all the roots along with the soil in which they will grow.

In this section we will deal with the Root in Rock style, as this is the simplest rock planting for a beginner. The essence of this style is to be able create a suitable pocket in the top or side of the chosen piece of rock in which the tree will be able to grow well. For a beginner, a piece of tufa, which is a very porous type of limestone, would be eminently suitable as a replacement for a harder type of rock as it is easy to carve with a chisel or spatula and therefore simple to excavate a hollow for the plants roots.

A small tree with a compact root ball is ideal for planting in a cavity or hollow in the rock. A layer of soil is placed in the cavity and the tree planted into the hollow, and firmed in. The hole is topped up with extra soil if required. This type of planting generally needs feeding more often than normal to maintain the health of the tree, as heavy rain and regular watering will wash nutrients away.

Below: An excellent example of a Root on Rock style of planting using Picea mariana *'Nana'.*

Above: This 15cm (6in) juvenile Chinese juniper has been removed from the plastic flower pot in which it was grown in a commercial nursery.

Advanced Techniques 83

Far left: Reduce the root ball in size so that it will fit into the cavity in the selected piece of porous rock.

Left: This is a suitable piece of weathered rock with a large crevice that will retain the plant nicely.

Left: Use your fingers to firm the plant's roots into the crevice of the rock.

Left: Remove any excess foliage to create the required image and place the rock onto a grit-filled pot. The grit will simulate water and give the overall appearance of an island in the sea. Place the pot on a wooden stand to further enhance the image (below).

Root over Rock

Root over Rock is style that is well worth trying. This style usually takes many years to prepare and is therefore not particularly suited to the beginner. Choose a tree with a suitably long root system and wash away all of the soil to expose the roots. Choose a piece of rock that has an interesting shape and spread the roots over it until they fit closely to the rock. Tie the roots tightly to the rock with string, raffia or wire. Wire will last longer and since the roots will take several years to mature it is the best choice. Plant the tree covering the whole root ball, including the rock, with soil. Throughout the next few years the roots will grow fitting closely to the rock so that when the rock is exposed, an interesting root system should have developed that follows the contours of the rock.

Creating Jin

In the wild, tree branches are ravaged by the natural elements, such as wind and rain, and sometimes break away leaving a dead stump. They are then bleached by the sun which gives them a natural silver-grey effect that eventually leads to a very aged appearance. This effect naturally occurs on many varieties of conifer, especially junipers and pines, and can be frequently seen on very old trees.

In bonsai this is referred to as 'jin'. Although jin does not normally appear on deciduous trees, it can often be seen on oak trees.

The reason for creating jin artificially on bonsai is to give the tree a real feeling of substantial age. When carried out correctly, a very dramatic effect can be achieved which will considerably enhance the appearance of the bonsai. If a branch on a conifer has to be removed for any reason, always leave about 20 to 30cm (8 to 12in) of growth on the tree so that it can be converted into a jin if required. The most suitable time of year in which to create jin is during the summer when the sap movement is at its peak. This makes the removal of the bark easier. Quite simply, to create a jin you just remove the bark from the remnant of the branch and allow it to dry naturally.

Having made the jin, leave it to dry in the sun before applying a coat of lime/sulphur which will bleach and preserve the exposed heartwood. This should be re-applied once or twice a year during the summer months to maintain the weather resistance of the jin. The jin can then be refined by carving and smoothing it with glass paper, until a truly natural effect is achieved. Remember that the jin you create must always be in proportion to the other branches remaining on the tree that bear foliage.

Left: Using sharp cutters, remove most of the branch leaving a short length (20-30cm/8-12in) from which to create the jin.

Above: Use a sharp knife to cut into the bark, down to the heartwood, around the junction of the branch and the trunk.

Advanced Techniques

Far left: Cut a narrow strip of bark from the junction, around the whole circumference of the branch.

Left: Slit the bark along the remaining length of the branch, using the sharp point of the knife.

Right: Using jinning pliers, or ordinary electrician's pliers, squeeze and twist the bark to free it from the heartwood beneath.

Right: Peel the loosened bark from the branch using the pliers.

Left: The bark has now been removed from the branch and the bare heartwood has been exposed.

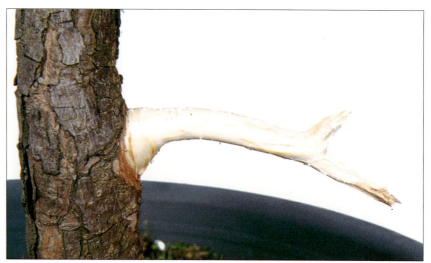

Above: Shape the tips of the jin to give it a natural weathered appearance using branch cutters or similar tools.

Above right: The completed jin should be allowed to dry naturally before applying a preserving and bleaching fluid, such as a mixture of lime and sulphur.

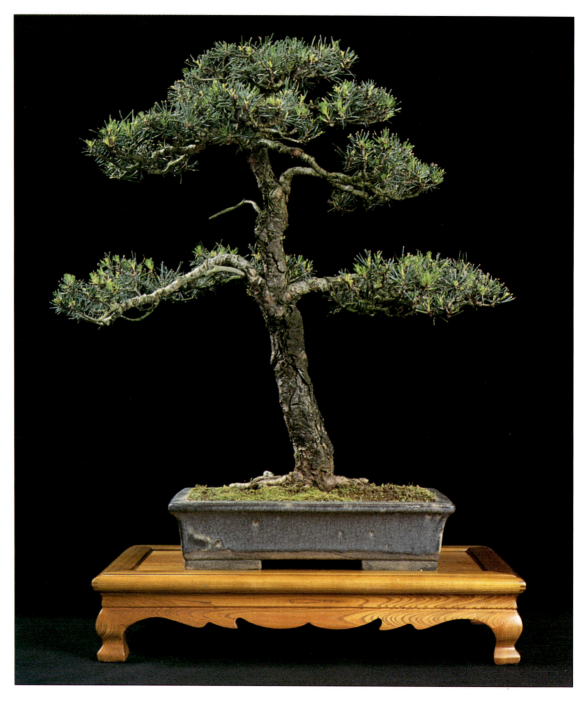

Right: Carefully prepared jin will help to give your bonsai the natural weathered appearance of an old tree. Use the technique sparingly and look at trees growing naturally to help you achieve an effect that is pleasing and convincing.

Creating Sharimiki

Sharimiki, usually known as 'shari' for short, is a technique which often complements a jin. It gives a tree an even greater appearance of age when a shari is used in conjunction with jin. A shari on a full-size tree is usually caused by a lightning strike when the bark on part of the trunk has been stripped off or when a branch is blown away in strong wind and falls down tearing the bark on the trunk as it falls. Again this is often seen on pines and junipers. It also often connects one jin with another, creating an even greater dramatic effect.

Sharis are created artificially for bonsai by stripping the bark from part of the trunk. This needs to be carried out with care because the tree depends upon its bark for survival. Enough bark must be left on the trunk to enable the tree to support its remaining branches. The stripped area of the trunk should be allowed to dry out naturally before being treated with lime/sulphur to preserve and bleach the heartwood. As with jin, the best time to make shari is during the summer when the sap is flowing at its greatest rate, therefore allowing the bark to be stripped easily. Over a period of time a shari can be refined by carving and sanding until a very mature, dramatic effect is formed.

Above: Using the tip of the knife, carefully peel away the bark in a downward direction.

Below: Draw the desired shape onto the trunk of the bonsai using a marker pen before starting to cut away the bark.

Above: Use a sharp knife to cut along the marked line through the bark to the heartwood of the tree.

Above: The completed sharimiki often looks better when it is linked to a jin. After allowing it to dry naturally, treat the cut area with a lime/sulphur mixture.

Collecting from the Wild

Some of the best pieces of material from which to design a bonsai can be found in your garden or in the wild. You may have a tree or shrub that you no longer require or come across a wild tree that could be suitable.

Look closely at your selected plant to see if it has the potential to become a bonsai, but before you dig up anything other than a plant from your own garden, you must obtain the landowner's permission. It is illegal to dig up any wild plant without the necessary authorization.

This type of plant, correctly worked, can lead to some of the best bonsai trees, as they often have very thick, mature trunks with a well-developed buttress as they have been growing unchecked for many years. Another source of suitable mature plants are old hedges, so you could be looking at a whole row of potential bonsai material. Look at the plants closely to see if they have a compact habit. If they have been clipped over many years, they could be ideal plants from which to start some new bonsai. Some species that are particularly suitable are azalea, beech, field maple, hedging honeysuckle, junipers, privet and many other varieties, all of which would be worth trying.

It may take one or more seasons to prepare these types of plants for removal from the ground. Being mature plants, they will have an extended root system that could spread out several metres from the trunk. You will need to cut through the roots with a spade in spring by plunging your spade into the soil around the plant to its full depth. Dig a circle with the spade around the trunk about 30 to 45cm (12-18in) from the base of the trunk before undercutting to sever any long taproots. The plant should be left for another season to develop a new compact root structure, and then dug out in the following spring, just before it starts into new growth. You may find it beneficial to do some initial pruning while the plant is still in the ground as this will help with the development of the basic structure. Collected trees should be planted into a training container using a very gritty open soil to encourage good fibrous root growth.

Use any type of container during this initial growing period. Make your own containers from

Left: The branches of this wild azalea have been cut for ease of transport and it has been planted in a temporary container.

Above: The unwanted overlapping secondary trunk is sawn off to create a simpler shape.

Advanced Techniques   89

any old timber or use washing bowls, plastic storage boxes or anything to hand that will contain the root ball of your plant. Do not forget to provide your home-made containers with large drainage holes in the base so that excess water can drain away freely. It may be necessary to tie the plant into the container so that the new roots can develop unhindered.

The plant used in this section was collected from a large bed of Satsuki azaleas that were due to be removed for replanting with different plants. Azaleas are excellent subjects for this type of operation as they have a close fibrous root structure and so are easy to dig up and repot without much risk to the plant. This specimen had been cut back whilst still in the ground but it required further surgery to turn it into a plant of great bonsai potential. A suitable pot will be chosen when the tree begins to show more maturity as it develops in its bonsai form.

Above left: A simpler outline has now been created.

Above: Using a saw, remove the top branches of the plant leaving the upper part of the trunk with just foliage.

Left: The lowest branch has now been removed and further unwanted branches are carefully trimmed away.

Above: The plant is ready to start life as a bonsai.

Chapter 6

Specimen Bonsai

Bonsai styling and growing can be extremely therapeutic and educational. It is a remarkably good way of understanding the growth patterns and requirements of a great variety of woody plants. It teaches you how to control the growth of plants as well how to respect them and to get the best out of them in terms of vigour, style and artistic expression. Take your time and experiment with various types of tree and a much fuller understanding will inevitably be the result.

Immediate success should not be expected as it can take time to master some of the general practices described, but with perseverance, a positive attitude and by using the techniques detailed previously in this book, spectacular results can be achieved. In the following pages you can see the result of some of the author's own work. You too can create effects like this and in the process find out just how rewarding the art of bonsai can be when the plants are correctly displayed in a complementary setting and against a suitable background.

Above: Acer palmatum *'Deshojo'*

94 The Beginner's Guide to Bonsai

Specimen Bonsai 95

Opposite: Acer palmatum *'Ukon'*

Above: Ulmus procera

Index

Acer buergerianum 78, 92
Acer palmatum 8, 17, 18, 42, 68-69, 78, 92, 95
Akadama 27, 34, 52, 81
aphid 60-61
azalea 16, 35, 88-89

bigleaf podocarp 66-67
bonsai culture 8, 11
bonsai exhibition 12
bonsai styles
    Cascade 20
    Driftwood 15, 21
    Informal Upright 14, 18
    Informal Upright Driftwood 14, 15
    Literati 21
    Multi-Trunk 18
    Root in Rock 21, 82
    Root on Rock 21, 82
    Root over Rock 21, 82, 83
    Semi-Cascade 15, 20
    Slanting 19
    Twin Trunk 18
bonsai tools 25, 28, 39
bonsai training 24, 48, 76
branch cutters/pruners 40, 46, 58, 86
brush 58, 60
Buxus sempervirens 17

Carpinus laxiflora 9
Cercidiphyllum japonicum 46
chopsticks 25, 27, 28, 50, 52, 56, 79, 81
'clip and grow' 44-45
coco brush 28, 59
collecting from the wild 88-89
compost 26, 27, 34-35
conifer 21, 27, 37, 41, 42, 47, 76, 84

cutters 25, 40, 43, 47, 49, 51, 64, 66, 84
cuttings 27, 66, 74
    heel 27

defoliating 42-43, 69
disease 50, 57, 58, 60-61, 66
drainage 30, 32, 34, 58, 79, 81, 89
dunking 55

elm 16, 45

feeding 35, 38, 42, 56-57, 71, 82
fertilizer 35, 37, 38, 56-57
Ficus benjamina 16, 70-71
forest planting 73, 78-81
full-size tree 8, 11, 16, 60, 63, 76, 87
fungicide 26, 27, 60

grafting 68, 73, 76-77
group planting 78-81
grub 60

hormone rooting powder 74

indoor bonsai 24, 54, 64, 66, 70
insecticide 60
insects 26, 58, 60-61

Japan Society of London 12
Japanese maple 68-69
jin 29, 41, 73, 84-86, 87
jinning pliers 29, 85
juniper 15, 16, 41, 43, 48, 84, 88
Juniper chinesis 17, 20, 82

Kanuma 35
Kasuga Shrine 12
Kiryu 35

knife 74, 84-85, 86
knob cutter 40, 51, 64
Kusumaki 66

layering 73, 74-75
Leonardslee Gardens 9
lime/sulphur mixture 84, 86, 87
liverwort 58

maintenance 58-59
mame 14
maple 15, 16, 26, 41, 48, 68-69, 88
mesh (plastic) 32-33, 79
misting 55, 71

Olea europea 64-65
olive, European 64-65
outdoor bonsai 24, 54, 66, 68, 79

pearlwort 58
peat substitute 34
Penjing 12
pests 39, 58, 60-61, 66
Picea mariana 82
pine 15, 16, 21, 38, 41, 48, 60, 84
rust 61
Podocarpus 16
    macrophyllus 66-67
pots 14, 21, 24, 30-31, 32-33, 52, 58, 64, 66, 69, 70, 78, 83, 89
potting 28, 37, 52, 65, 69, 70, 75
propagation 26, 27, 66, 74
pruning 18, 37, 38, 40-41, 46-47, 52, 63, 64, 69, 70, 88
shears 28
pyracantha 20

rake 28, 50
'ready-made' bonsai 8

repotting 38, 50-51, 52-53
Rhododendron obtusum 19
rock planting 12, 73, 82-83
root hook 28, 50
root pruning 50-51, 52-53, 63, 66, 69, 70

Saigyo Momogatari Emaki 12
scale insect 60-61
sealer 40, 46, 76
seed 26, 74
sharamiki 73, 87
shohin 14
sieve 28, 35
slab (slate or rock) 78
soil 34-35
specimen bonsai 90-95
sphagnum moss 34, 74-75
spraying 55, 56, 58

tools 28, 29
traditional bonsai 14
transpiration 27, 51, 55
trimming 37, 38, 44, 46, 79
tufa 82

Ulmus procera 95

vine weevil 60-61

watering 14, 26, 39, 43, 52, 54-55, 56, 63, 71, 81, 82
weeping fig 70-71
Windsor Castle 12
wire 18, 23, 29, 32, 34, 37, 48-49, 52, 69, 76-77, 78, 83
wire cutters 29
wiring 29, 48-49, 52, 63, 69, 76-77

Zelkova serrata 74

Awesome ANIMALS

Steve Parker
Consultant: Camilla de la Bedoyere

Miles Kelly

Unusual Moves

All animals need to move to find food, seek shelter, escape enemies, and of course link up with breeding partners. Most creatures walk, run, fly, or swim, depending on their habitat, but some use unusual and unexpected ways of moving—such as flying with their feet!

Feet feats

From cheetahs and deer to ostriches and cockroaches, long, slim legs are a sure sign of speedy sprinters. There are many ways to get about on foot—kangaroos hop, grasshoppers leap, fleas jump, and some lizards and bugs even walk on water. However, few creatures are bipedal (move around regularly on two legs). A lizard may rear up briefly in fear, and an orangutan might amble along a branch, but only a select few—birds and humans—have the upright posture and delicate balance for bipedal walking.

▲ The sifaka, a large Madagascan lemur, holds out its arms for balance while it moves using short, sideways hops.

▲ The mudskipper uses its muscular armlike pectoral fins to haul its body across the tidal ooze. If in danger, this bizarre fish flips its whole body into the air to move to safety.

CONTENTS

Unusual Moves	6
Cool Senses	8
The Gross Factor	10
Wicked Assassins	12
Deadly Defense	14
Young and Old	16
Dinner Time	18
The Perfect Animal?	20
Buddies vs Baddies	22
Showtime Spectacular!	24
Bright Sparks	26
Strength in Numbers	28
Strange Babies	30
Brilliant Builders	32
Super Strength	34
Can You See Me?	36
The Big Lineup	38
Index	40

◀ The red-eyed tree frog has a thin membrane that partly covers its brightly colored eye. This allows the frog to see while remaining camouflaged.

◀ Frogs usually use their webbed feet to provide a powerful push when swimming. However, the flying frog of Southeast Asia sails through the air using its webs like mini-parachutes to increase drag, slowing its descent.

Emergency aerobats

There's a massive difference between actual flying, like a bird, and a perilous leap into midair with just flaps of skin preventing a fatal plummet to the ground. "Flying" squirrels, lizards, frogs, and snakes don't actually fly, but glide. Their aerial ability is mainly used for emergencies. They create a broad surface, often by opening out flaps of skin, which encounters air resistance to slow their fall. A tilt or twist gives some control over direction, and a few bruises on landing are preferable to being gobbled up by a predator.

CLOCKED AT MORE THAN 65 MPH (105 KM/H), THE SAILFISH IS THE FASTEST SWIMMER IN THE WORLD.

▶ Using its partly webbed toes and fast strides, the basilisk lizard races on its hind legs across water—with no time to sink.

Water sports

Muscle-packed bodies and thrashing fins give fish speed—the fastest species, such as the sailfish, have stiff, narrow, crescent-shaped tails. However, fins are adaptable and can be used for out-of-water movement, too, such as in the goby and walking catfish. Bird wings are similar in shape to fins and some birds use them to thrust through water rather than air. Kingfishers and dippers can "swim" briefly, but penguins have given up air flight completely and only "fly" underwater.

▲ The kingfisher, using its wings as both rudders and underwater brakes, strikes with astonishing accuracy.

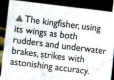

COOL Senses

All around are more light rays, sounds, and smells than humans could ever imagine. Animals of all kinds can tune into this abundance of sensations with their amazing supersenses. Often an animal is almost entirely dependent on just one dominant sense—block a bat's ears or an anteater's nostrils and they cannot survive.

▶ Giant anteaters sniff out their tiny quarry from more than 150 ft (45 m) away.

▼ The male cockchafer beetle's feathery antennae (feelers) detect scent particles, called pheromones, from females up to several miles away. These pheromone messages tell the male that the females are ready to mate.

Sniff, snort, snuffle

A polar bear can sniff out a seal carcass up to 4.5 mi (7 km) away, while a human would need to be within 300 ft (90 m) to detect even a trace of this rotting stench. Bears, wolves, and dogs far exceed a human's capacity because they have more than 200 million microscopic smell cells in their noses, compared to a human's five million. The sense of smell is not just for finding food. Without it, elephants would die of thirst, lions would not be able to mark their territory, and many moths and beetles could never detect scents released by potential mates that tell them they are ready to breed.

ANIMALS VS HUMANS

RHINO Sight estimated at five times poorer than a human's—it cannot distinguish between another rhino and a jeep at 300 ft (90 m) away. However, its sense of smell is ten times better than a human's.

EAGLE Sight is at least ten times better than a human's—it can see a rabbit more than 2 mi (3 km) away.

BAT Hearing can pick up vibrations ten times faster than a human—so it can hear a tiny gnat's flapping wings.

MOTH Sense of smell is more than 10,000 times more sensitive than a human's—it can scent nectar from a blossom that a human could not even see in daylight!

▲ A bat finds its way around using echolocation—it squeaks and then listens to the echoes to work out where objects in its path are. Large ears help a bat to gather these sounds. If a human's ears were relative in size to the long-eared bat's, they would be bigger than trashcan lids!

Hear, hear!

A noise that sounds quiet to a human might deafen an owl or a bat. They have far more microsensors in their ears, and they move their ears or head much more carefully to receive the maximum number of sound waves and pinpoint an object's position. Ears are not always on the head. Insects such as grasshoppers and crickets have them on their knees, and some fish "hear" with their swim bladders.

Seeing the invisible

Animal eyes can see infrared and ultraviolet light—both of which are outside the spectrum of light that is visible to humans. Insects in particular are highly tuned to these invisible wavelengths. To a bee, plain-looking petals are covered with ultraviolet lines that point to the sweet nectar inside. Some fish have an amazing sense of sight, too. Piranhas can see the warm, infrared glow of a mammal—then launch their mass attack.

▲ Finding and attacking prey is no problem for a jumping spider. They have two huge eyes to see objects in great detail and color. The remaining six eyes detect movement and create a large field of vision.

The GROSS Factor

Animals have some disgusting habits. To deter predators, they spray vomit or excrement, spit saliva, and even squirt blood from open vessels. When it comes to feeding, they certainly have no manners—tearing at flesh and creating a bloody mess. Some animals even tuck into excrement for a tasty snack.

THE HORNED LIZARD SQUIRTS A BLOODY FLUID FROM ITS EYES—MORE THAN 5 FT (1.5 M)—AT A THREAT.

Disgusting defense

Vomit, slime, urine, droppings, spit, and pus can sting, cause infection, and create an off-putting stench. Some animals capitalize on this by using their bodily fluids to make enemies recoil and retreat. The innocent-looking sea cucumber throws up its super-sticky guts over an attacker, while several kinds of seabird projectile vomit more than 3 ft (1 m) at an enemy.

▼ The world's largest lizards have big appetites. Komodo dragons feast on a rotting dolphin carcass, enjoying the fatty blubber and the guts filled with semidigested fish. Male komodos can reach lengths of 10 ft (3 m).

Feeding frenzy

Even before a huge pile of food becomes available, predators and scavengers wait in the wings. A dying whale is tracked by sharks, orcas, and seabirds, while a sick elephant lures hyenas, jackals, and vultures. As soon as one plucks up the courage to move in for a mouthful, the rest rush to grab what they can. The feeding frenzy that follows is rough, gory, and urgent as they push and scrap to get the best share before it's all gone.

Messy breeders

Animal babies can be born in the most disgusting conditions. Some parasitic wasp grubs hatch in the guts of a caterpillar, and proceed to eat the host alive. Dung beetle grubs emerge from their eggs into balls of excrement. Surinam toad tadpoles develop inside their mother's back, under her skin. Other frogs whip up a foam using a cocktail of their saliva, skin slime, sperm fluid, and excrement, and lay their eggs here.

▼ A group of male gray foam-nest tree frogs cluster around one female and whip their bodily fluids into a froth, in which she deposits her spawn.

Nasty nourishment

Dung, droppings, and excrement might look and smell horrible. However, the digestion of most animals is not very efficient, so feces often still contain plenty of nutrients. Dung eaters usually like to get it while it's fresh, before molds, germs, and flies arrive to contaminate the rotting mass.

▲ This turkey vulture quickly devours fishy feces from a fur seal.

Wicked ASSASSINS

Natural born killers are feared for their deadly weapons. These fearsome animals mercilessly slay their prey with lethal teeth, claws, and fangs, devouring flesh, bones, and blood with ease—no morsel is spared.

Wolfie the Wolffish

Last seen in the waters of the Atlantic Ocean, the wolffish is 5 ft (1.5 m) long and can be recognized by its vast number of teeth. It has about 100 of them—fanglike at the front, broad for crushing at the back, and continuing into its throat. Its typical victims are shellfish, starfish, crabs, and urchins, which the wolffish crushes to death with great power.

WANTED

Terminator the Alligator

This 15-ft- (4.6-m-) long 'gator is wanted for drowning prey by dragging it underwater. Victims include turtles, snakes, waterbirds, and mammals up to the size of deer. Beware—the alligator is armed and dangerous, with 50 cone-shaped teeth and amazingly strong jaw muscles. Do not approach.

WANTED
REWARD $2,000

JAWS the Grizzly Bear

Towering up to 10 (3 m) tall, the grizzly a formidable hunte Its weapons include powerful teeth and jaws plate-sized paws, and curved claws. These features, combined with enormous weight, power, and stamina, mean that nothing is safe. The grizzly will attack anything up to the size of moose and never lets go.

FANG THE GABOON VIPER

The Gaboon viper is a massive 6 ft (2 m) long. Mice, rats, birds, and similar small creatures have been found dead, marked with puncture wounds. This cold-blooded killer strikes at lightning speed, using its long, foldout front fangs to stab the victim's flesh and inject deadly venom. It then waits for the victim to die of shock as the heart stops beating (cardiac arrest).

WANTED
DEAD OR ALIVE

SMILER THE SAND TIGER SHARK

Lurking in the shadows of the deep, the 11-ft- (3.5-m-) long sand tiger shark charges suddenly, taking its victim by surprise. Fish, squid, shellfish, and crabs have all suffered from this menace's slashing bite.

MOST WANTED

CLAWS THE LION

A master of stealth, this 8-ft- (2.4-m-) long assassin camouflages itself among the grass, stalking before the sudden rush of attack. Armed with huge canine teeth and slicing back teeth, victims are killed with a throat-crushing bite, before the lion tears its flesh apart using sharp, curved claws. An experienced killer, no "hit" is too big or small for this ferocious feline. Its kill list includes gazelles and antelope, as well as rats and beetles.

BABOONS OFTEN KILL OTHER BABOONS TO BECOME THE BOSS OF THE TROOP.

Deadly DEFENSE

The forest is nearly dark and almost quiet. A creature sneaks up on the juicy meal it has been tracking. It steadies itself, preparing to pounce... WOAH! Suddenly two huge eyes appear, glaring in the gloom. A big cat? A snake? An owl? No, they're eyespots (false eyes)—one of many animal self-defense tactics.

Terrible taste

Having horrible-tasting or poisonous flesh deters predators and works as a great group defense strategy. After biting one foul-tasting animal, a hunter learns to recognize its warning signs, such as colors and patterns, and stays away from all similar-looking prey.

◀ The African foam grasshopper shows its nasty taste by blowing noxious bubbles from tiny breathing holes, called spiracles, along its body.

Animal armor

Some creatures lack speed to escape enemies, or foul-tasting defenses to deter them. Instead they use simple physical protection. Tough-shelled animals include crabs, clams, and snails, as well as armadillos and pangolins. They simply shut up tight and wait for the danger to pass.

▶ The three-banded armadillo has bony plates within its skin, covered by outer scales of horny keratin. Its armor is so flexible that it can curl into a tight ball that will completely defeat predators.

◀ A rear view of the peacock katydid (a type of grasshopper) shows how its suddenly raised wings display enormous eyespots to startle a potential attacker.

PLAYING DEAD
When under threat, the Virginia opossum flops onto its side, puts out its tongue, leaks foul-smelling anal fluid, and emits a rotting stench. By acting "dead," no hunter will try to eat it.

Guns blazing
Camouflage is a great defense tactic. An animal that matches the background color of its habitat can just sit still and hope to go unnoticed. But what if it's spotted? The next tactic is to make a grand show of defense—rear up, look big, reveal your weapons, make a noise, wave and shake, and generally try to look as frightening and inedible as possible.

▶ If its disguise is rumbled, the dead-leaf mantis raises its body and extends its wings and fearsome, spiked, jackknife forelegs to appear super-fierce.

Young and Old

Why do elephants live longer than flies? These creatures are at two ends of a whole spectrum of life strategies. One is to develop slowly, and take great care of just a few young. The other is to live fast and die young, mating frequently and producing lots of offspring but providing no parental care.

4 MONTHS

Congratulations!

Labord's chameleon
Shortest-lived of any four-legged vertebrate, this lizard's life cycle is perfectly adapted to Madagascar's seasonal changes. It lives for a single year, spending eight months in an egg and just four months in its adult form.

1 DAY!

Have a Great Day!

happy birthday! 1 TODAY!

Brine shrimp
Old shrimps lay tough-cased eggs before their salt lake dries up for summer. When it starts to rain in fall, the eggs hatch, and the next generation begins to feed.

Mayfly
The mayfly spends a year or two as an underwater nymph. Then it emerges, molts to reveal its wonderful wings, mates in midair, and dies—all within 24 hours.

Worker honeybee
Day after day of nonstop toil means the worker honeybee's body suffers immense wear and tear. The egg-laying queen might make it to five years old.

I AM 3 WEEKS OLD

Bee Happy!

Dinner Time

In the wild, animals rarely know where their next meal is coming from, so any snack is greedily gobbled up. If a glut of food appears, some species will eat until they are almost bursting—the opportunity to devour their fill may not come again.

▶ The Bryde's whale spends all day filtering tiny creatures such as krill and small fish from the water. Its daily diet can weigh 3 tons—equivalent to the amount of food eaten by a human over a period of seven or eight years.

▼ This African bullfrog has no teeth and cannot tear up or chew its mouse victim. Instead, frogs and toads feed by stretching their head-wide mouths and gulping prey whole.

Down in one

The bodies of many creatures are adapted for eating huge amounts in a single feeding session. Features range from a stretchy stomach to a dislocating jaw. With scavengers and enemies lurking everywhere, fast food is best—rapid gulps or the all-in-one swallow. After gorging their fill, these gluttons can hide away from danger while they digest.

Leave it in the larder

Some animals store excess food for later, to avoid waste and prepare for periods when food is scarce. Squirrels bury nuts, crocodiles wedge gazelles beneath underwater rocks, and tigers scrape leaves and soil over deer carcasses. These clever methods mean these creatures are less likely to die of starvation when times are hard.

▶ The leopard can haul a kill three times its own weight up into a tree, away from scavengers such as jackals.

▼ These white-backed vultures rush to peck the juiciest morsels from a dead giraffe, before pack of hyenas arrive on the scene.

Scavenger hunt

Old meat is still a valuable source of nourishment, so a large carcass attracts a multitude of scavengers. The first (airborne vultures) and the fiercest (hyena clans) get the richest pickings. Lesser scavengers such as jackals soon follow.

Bite to kill

Any predator must make careful decisions about which prey to tackle, and how. If an animal has just eaten, it may feel full and sluggish, and this might put it off tackling another large victim. A predator will also assess the fitness of potential prey—is it strong and healthy, or (preferably) too young, old, or sick, for its defenses to prove a problem? The attack itself must be swift and decisive, since in the wild even a slight injury makes a hunter far less capable.

▶ After a lightning, twist-and-turn chase, the leopard seal strikes with its viciously sharp canine teeth. The seal moves in as the penguin weakens, and chomps away at the fatty blubber and tasty flesh.

The Perfect Animal?

Every species is superbly adapted to its habitat and way of life. But some creatures' features are super-adapted, compared to other, similar animals. If we could bring together all these extreme adaptations into one combi-creature, surely it would instantly be crowned king of the animal kingdom?

Ringtailed lemur's TAIL
Not only an excellent balance aid, the lemur's tail is used to convey signals about mood and intention. The male sprays a nasty scent on its own tail and waves it at opponents to mark its territory. The tail also indicates an individual's rank within the group, and attracts a mate.

Cheetah's BODY
Slim and streamlined, the fastest land animal's body is lithe yet muscular and flexible, and ideal for out-sprinting prey.

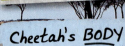

Gerenuk's HIND LEGS
Slim and strong, this antelope rears up on its hind legs to reach juicy leaves in tall trees—food that few other animals can reach.

Elephant's EARS
Not only brilliant for catching faint sounds, the world's biggest ears can flap both to lose internal heat and to fan cooling air over the body.

Tarsier's EYES
The tarsier hunts by grabbing passing moths and bats, so its massive eyes have a fabulous ability to follow fast motion, as well as superb vision even on the darkest nights.

Tiger's MOUTH
Huge, sharp teeth and one of the biggest, strongest bites of any land animal ensures that any victim is fatally wounded in an instant.

Proboscis monkey's NOSE
Long and drooping, this remarkable nose amplifies hoots and calls, and also offers a superior sense of smell compared to other monkey species.

Giraffe's NECK
As well as reaching far higher food than any other ground-bound animal, a giraffe's excellent vantage point gives it an all-round aerial view—so it can spot approaching predators from a long way off.

Kangaroo's LEGS
The kangaroo's hind legs offer an energy-efficient, bouncing gait, with the added extra of huge leaps 26 ft (8 m) long and 13 ft (4 m) high.

The natural world is both nice and nasty, when animals of two different species live together in a symbiotic relationship. Here, both partners help each other in some way for mutual benefit.

Best of friends

Sea anemones and clownfish work together in harmony. Although anemones feed by paralyzing small fish with their stinging tentacles, the clownfish's slimy coating resists the venom. The anemone recognizes this and rarely attempts to attack. In return for this safe haven, the clownfish eats debris and pests among the tentacles to keep the anemone clean. The anemone also scares off animals that may prey on clownfish, while the clownfish lures in other fish to be eaten by the anemone.

▶ As the clownfish swims around the anemone, water circulation increases, which helps the anemone to breathe.

▶ Ants crowd around the aphids and "milk" them so they secrete sweet, sugar-rich honeydew.

Buddies vs Baddies

Sometimes partnerships are horribly one-sided. One benefits, while the other gets hurt—the parasite-host situation. But being a parasite is a balancing act. If you are too successful, all your hosts die out and you have nowhere to live and nothing to eat.

Eaten alive

Some of the nastiest parasites are small wasps that lay their eggs in living caterpillars and other larvae. The wasp stings and paralyzes the caterpillar, then deposits its eggs inside the host's body. The wasp grubs hatch and proceed to eat the helpless host bit by bit.

▼ This tomato hornworm caterpillar is covered with parasitic wasp eggs. Its death will be slow as the hatched grubs chomp away until all that's left is an empty skin.

Protection for food

Aphids (greenfly and blackfly) are tiny, soft, and defenseless—except when they are in the care of an ant colony. While the aphids feed on plant sap with their sucking mouthparts, ants from a nearby nest patrol the region and keep away aphid enemies, such as ladybugs. In return for their protection, the ants feed on a sugary liquid, called honeydew, produced by the aphids.

▼ This impala is being "cleaned" by red-billed oxpeckers. Although they get rid of pests, oxpeckers may also peck at their host's skin, keeping wounds open—making this bird both a helper and a parasite.

A quick cleanup

The oxpecker doesn't only peck oxen—it may debug antelope, gazelles, giraffes, zebras, rhinos… as well as many more. The bird feeds on pests, such as lice, fleas, and ticks, especially in hard-to-reach places, as well as blood from any open wounds.

▶ This common cuckoo fledgling dwarfs its eager dunnock foster parent. The dunnock's instinct to feed its young is so strong, it fails to recognize that this giant youngster is an imposter.

Crafty cuckoo

A brood parasite takes advantage of other animals at breeding time, using them to raise its own offspring. The female cuckoo lays her egg in another bird's nest. The chick hatches, pushes out the other eggs, and demands food from its new parents. Other brood parasites include cowbirds, whydahs, and honeyguides.

SHOWTIME Spectacular!

Rivals for attention
Impressing partners is only a part of courtship. Animals may also have to compete with rivals who want to get in on the action and steal their partner.

M ost creatures spend their time keeping a low profile, trying to stay unnoticed by predators. But there are times when an animal needs to make itself known, showing off any special features, either to attract a mate or to discourage a rival or enemy from approaching.

FLICKER, FLASH
The female **glowworm** is actually a wingless beetle and glows to attract a winged male for mating.

DRESS UP
A male **ruff** erects his beautiful soft collar of pale feathers as he struts and calls when breeding.

KICK, PUNCH
A female **hare** plays hard to get as she "boxes" with a male to test his health, speed, reactions, and vigor.

BLOW UP
A male **greater frigate** stretches his gular (throat) pouch to show his potential as a mating partner.

Courting couples

Animal courtship is not just a quick flirt for fun—it's a serious test. Each partner checks the other is the correct species, strong and healthy, and will pass on good genes to any offspring.

FAN OUT
A **peacock** fans out his shimmering, green tail to impress a peahen. The brighter the colors, the more attractive his tail appears.

FEED ME
A **European bee-eater** pair give each other food morsels as they flutter like butterflies when courting.

PUFF OUT
The male **hooded seal** impresses potential partners by inflating a balloon of skin out of its nose.

FLAG UP
A courting male **anole lizard** flicks out his colorful throat fan, or dewlap, to attract a mate.

Bright SPARKS

Q: What do chimps, dolphins, octopuses, elephants, parrots, dogs, and monkeys have in common?

A: They are some of the animal world's smartest cookies. Their range of talents—including tool use, problem solving, and teamwork—make them top of the class.

Using tools

Many animals have developed incredible techniques to obtain food otherwise unattainable for them. The Egyptian vulture uses a stone as a hammer to crack a tough egg, while the woodpecker finch extracts grubs from tree holes with a cactus spine. The master is the chimp—it not only uses tools, but also modifies them. For example, it chews the end of its termite "fishing stick" to make it sleeker and easier to poke into the mound.

The Egyptian vulture drops a stone onto an ostrich egg to break it open and feed on the nutritious contents.

Chimps have developed a clever way to collect termites. They poke a stem into a termite nest, then simply withdraw it and lick off the termites.

This veined octopus carries a discarded cockle shell for shelter.

Problem solving
Problem: if you are soft-bodied, how do you guard against hungry enemies? Solution: borrow someone else's protection. The hermit crab uses this technique and will try on several old whelk shells for size to find the best fit. Small fish and octopuses also take advantage of empty seashells as temporary shelters.

Dolphins "talk" using clicks and squeaks as they corral sardines into a baitball, where they can be picked off easily.

SPECIAL STORAGE
The acorn woodpecker slots acorns and other nuts into purpose-pecked bark cracks, adding more holes each year.

Weaver ants divide into teams to make their nests. One team holds the leaf edges together with their jaws, while a second team makes the ant larvae produce silk, which is then used to "sew" the leaf edges together.

Dream team
Each member of an animal team knows its place and its purpose within the group. Ants are preprogrammed to only follow a few simple instincts, so rarely adapt to new situations. With a decreasing fish population in the oceans, dolphins, however, have developed new methods of finding food—such as chasing trawler nets laden with fish, to feed on any escapees.

Strength in NUMBERS

Living and working together in a group can offer some species many advantages. With more animals, there is a greater number of resources—more eyes on the lookout, more defensive weapons to protect the young, and more teeth and claws to attack prey.

Mighty migration

Animals go on annual or seasonal journeys, called migrations, usually due to changes in climate or a seasonal lack of food. Every year, at the start of the wet season (October–November), Christmas Island red crabs move across the shore like an unstoppable red tide, marching into the sea to lay eggs in their millions.

Body building

An inconvenient gap in the path is no problem for a swarming ant colony, especially when they are army ants on the march. The ants simply build a bridge from their own bodies. Neighboring ants lock legs as more climb over them to lengthen the interlinked chains. The bridging ants may stay like this for hours, and even die, as their fellow workers surge over and resume the search for fresh food.

Savage swarms

Locusts require a few months of good conditions to breed and build up their numbers. Gradually, they form an enormous gathering, capable of completely consuming vegetation across an entire region. Continuously in search of fresh greenery, swarms containing hundreds of millions of locusts can quickly ravage farm crops.

Hound dogs

African wild dogs can take down large prey, up to 20 times their own size—using teamwork. The lead dog picks out a young, old, or sick quarry such as a wildebeest. With dogged determination the pack hounds the desperate victim for many miles, until it is so weak from exhaustion that they can move in for the kill.

ANY HINT OF BLOOD IN THE WATER SENDS A GROUP OF RED-BELLIED PIRANHAS INTO A FEEDING FRENZY. WITH DOZENS OF SETS OF RAZOR-SHARP SLASHING TEETH, THEIR FEROCIOUS ATTACK IS IMMEDIATE AND OFTEN FATAL.

Strange Babies

Many animal parents have strong caring instincts, and will even risk their lives to save their babies. Some creatures go to extremes to give their offspring the best chance of survival. The young of some species are born while still at an early stage of development, when they are vulnerable and require constant care. They also look nothing like their parents—in fact, some animal babies look very odd indeed.

▼ A female giant panda gives birth to a single cub, which may stay with her for two years or more. Once a cub is weaned (after the first year), the mother may leave it for days at a time, while she forages for food.

Mini me or metamorphosis?

Some animal offspring, such as seal pups and tiger cubs, are unmistakable mini versions of their parents. Others, such as tadpoles and caterpillars, change dramatically from birth to adulthood. These drastic changes in shape, called metamorphoses, allow the youngsters to live in different environments and eat different foods from the parents, to avoid competing against each other.

Pink and hairless

Many newborn mammals and birds are born when they are still pink and hairless. Their eyes and ears are closed, and they can only feed and sleep. The mother can leave them to find food for herself—once the youngsters are hidden in a nest or a burrow. Her offspring are entirely dependent on her for protection and food.

◀▲ Most caterpillars hatch from eggs a few days after they are laid. They consume vast amounts of leaves before pupating inside a chrysalis and emerging in their adult form to feed on flower nectar.

▼ Seal cubs look just like their parents, except they are born with white fur. They feed on their mother's rich milk and grow faster than any other mammal of their size.

▶ A newborn kangaroo doesn't have proper arms or legs. Yet straight away it has to climb from the birth opening and through its mother's fur to her pouch. Then it attaches to a teat, and stays there for six months until ready to leave the pouch.

Born at an early age

Marsupial mammals such as kangaroos, koalas, wombats, and possums are born at a very early stage of development. Many do not even have recognizable eyes or ears, and their limbs are just flaps or "buds" on the featureless body. These newborns do little except wriggle to the mother's pouch, or marsupium, latch onto a teat with their barely formed mouth, and feed on her milk. Within the protection of the pouch, they continue the stages of development that other mammals go through while still in the womb.

▶ The Virginia opossum may have more tiny pink babies (below) than she has teats. Some die so that the survivors can grow big enough for a ride (above).

Brilliant Builders

Animals create some amazing structures, whether building alone or in groups. Everything they build is for a purpose—a nest to protect their young, a bridge to get from one place to another, or a trap to capture prey. Building methods can vary, depending on what materials are available in a particular habitat.

Supersize it

Some creatures make massive constructions compared to their size. Termites are insects that are only the size of peas, yet their mounds can tower more than 32 ft (10 m) high—that's equivalent to a skyscraper more than 1.5 mi (2.5 km) tall. Other outsizers dig down deep. A network of tunnels built by prairie dogs in Texas, U.S., covered 23,000 sq mi (60,000 sq km) and housed 400 million of these rodents—20 times more people than in the largest cities.

◀ Much of the termite mound above the ground is hollow chimneys, made of sun-baked earth. They provide air-conditioning to the main nest below ground level.

Adult human

20-ft termite mound

◀ The masked weaver tears leaves and stems into strips and delicately intertwines them to create its ball- or flask-shaped nest.

Perfect homemakers

Animals often build nests or burrows to live in for just a short time, usually to raise their young. Most of their behavior is instinctive, but skills and techniques improve greatly with practice. Nests can be made out of a wide range of natural materials, such as grass and mud, as well as materials from other animals, such as feathers and fur.

▶ The breeding nest of the harvest mouse is hardly larger than a tennis ball. It is built in between stems, high above the ground, to protect the young from danger.

◀▼ A beaver lodge can reach up to 65 ft (20 m) wide and 16 ft (5 m) high.

My home is my castle

The beaver's house, or lodge, is a solid construction of branches, rocks, twigs, and mud. Each generation of beavers carefully fells trees, gnaws off boughs, and adds reinforcements to make an amazing fortress that even hungry wolves and bears cannot break into.

Super STRENGTH

Heavyweight

Elephants can lift logs and other objects weighing up to one ton with their trunks—but the elephant has a great body weight, too, at 5 tons. So a fairer measure of strength is to compare weight moved against body weight—for an elephant, this is just 1/5.

◀ Elephants are the strongest of all land animals, but that's mainly due to their great size.

AN ELEPHANT CAN LIFT ONE FIFTH OF ITS OWN BODY WEIGHT.

Human weightlifters can hoist more than three times their body weight, but that's puny compared to some insects. We are weaklings in other ways too, like our jumping ability, pulling power, or bite strength. But we are champions in one way— as athletic all-rounders.

A WEASEL CAN LIFT 30 TIMES MORE THAN ITS OWN BODY WEIGHT.

Weasels are the world's smallest carnivores, with some individuals weighing little more than one ounce (30 g). They must eat at least one third of their own body weight every day to survive, and can bring down rabbits weighing 35 oz (one kilogram) or more.

A DUNG BEETLE CAN PULL MORE THAN 1,000 TIMES ITS OWN BODY WEIGHT.

▼ Dung beetles can roll balls of fresh dung up to 30 times more than their own body weight.

ANTS CAN LIFT UP TO 50 TIMES MORE THAN THEIR OWN BODY WEIGHT AND CAN CARRY THE LOAD OVER A DISTANCE OF MANY FEET.

Rolling home

Dung beetles roll excrement—from animals including rhinos, wolves, antelopes, elephants, and cats—into balls. While the dung is still moist, the beetles roll the balls to a suitable place, lay eggs inside them, and bury them. The grubs then feed on the dung when they hatch.

A SHARK CAN BITE 60 TIMES HARDER THAN A HUMAN.

Bite size

Bite power depends on whether the biter is angry or relaxed, and whether it uses all its teeth and jaws. Lions, hyenas, sharks, and crocodiles are all super-crunchers, able to crush the bones of prey with ease. However, the extinct dinosaur *T rex* probably had the strongest bite of any animal that has ever lived.

▶ Great white sharks have a strong bite, but the real damage comes from its razor-sharp teeth that can easily saw through flesh and bone.

Can You See Me?

One of the oldest tricks in the animal world is for your body shape, color, pattern, or texture to mimic your surroundings. Camouflage is all about visual trickery and blending in, whether it's to stay unnoticed by enemies or lurk unseen near prey.

A broken-off tree stump merits no second look. Just as well for the great potoo, a night-hunting bird that must stay completely still by day.

Acting the part

Camouflage depends not only on colors, patterns, and shapes, but on movements, too. It's no good merging perfectly into the surroundings, if a sudden movement gives the game away. To be successful, camouflaged creatures must move with extreme care. If the leaf it is resting on blows in the wind, the animal must hang on and sway with it, or risk discovery.

The imperial moth is highly camouflaged on the forest floor, and must rustle and flip with the real leaf litter.

To remain concealed, the leaf-tail gecko must mimic the random motion of a dead leaf—whether remaining motionless or moving with the breeze.

Peering faces

Some predators are not so much well camouflaged as well hidden. Forest frogs, desert toads, and soil-dwelling spiders burrow into the ground, leaving only their eyes and ears exposed to detect passing prey. They must stay like this for hours, until their victim relaxes and strays within reach of their lightning strike.

The Chacoan horned frog almost buries itself in soil, waiting for a beetle or grub to pass by.

A SHARK'S COLORING HELPS IT TO SNEAK UP ON PREY—ITS DARK BACK BLENDS WITH THE SEABED, WHILE ITS PALE BELLY MATCHES THE LIGHTER WATER ABOVE. THIS IS KNOWN AS "COUNTERSHADING."

The nose and eyes of the sidewinding adder match the grains of desert sand around it, hiding it almost completely from view as it waits patiently for its next victim.

Lurking danger

The bigger you are, the more difficult it is to hide from your prey. Big cats have some of the best camouflage colors and patterns, with each species well adapted to its main habitat. Lions are tawny to match the African savanna's dry grasses and dusty soils. Tiger stripes blend in with undergrowth and shrubs, and are particularly effective in the half-light when they are usually out hunting. Leopards and jaguars tend to stay among trees, and their spots mimic the dappled shadows cast by the twigs and leaves above.

A lion peers through the African grassland, perfectly color-matched to its surroundings, on the lookout for food—and danger.

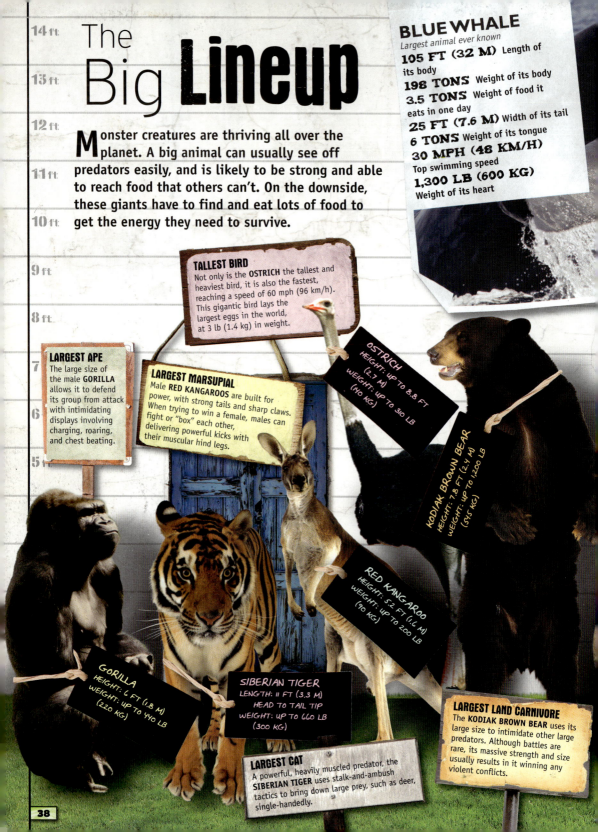

The Big Lineup

Monster creatures are thriving all over the planet. A big animal can usually see off predators easily, and is likely to be strong and able to reach food that others can't. On the downside, these giants have to find and eat lots of food to get the energy they need to survive.

BLUE WHALE
Largest animal ever known
- **105 FT (32 M)** Length of its body
- **198 TONS** Weight of its body
- **3.5 TONS** Weight of food it eats in one day
- **25 FT (7.6 M)** Width of its tail
- **6 TONS** Weight of its tongue
- **30 MPH (48 KM/H)** Top swimming speed
- **1,300 LB (600 KG)** Weight of its heart

TALLEST BIRD
Not only is the **OSTRICH** the tallest and heaviest bird, it is also the fastest, reaching a speed of 60 mph (96 km/h). This gigantic bird lays the largest eggs in the world, at 3 lb (1.4 kg) in weight.

LARGEST APE
The large size of the male **GORILLA** allows it to defend its group from attack with intimidating displays involving charging, roaring, and chest beating.

LARGEST MARSUPIAL
Male **RED KANGAROOS** are built for power, with strong tails and sharp claws. When trying to win a female, males can fight or "box" each other, delivering powerful kicks with their muscular hind legs.

OSTRICH
HEIGHT: UP TO 8.8 FT (2.7 M)
WEIGHT: UP TO 310 LB (140 KG)

KODIAK BROWN BEAR
HEIGHT: 7.8 FT (2.4 M)
WEIGHT: UP TO 1200 LB (545 KG)

RED KANGAROO
HEIGHT: 5.2 FT (1.6 M)
WEIGHT: UP TO 200 LB (90 KG)

GORILLA
HEIGHT: 6 FT (1.8 M)
WEIGHT: UP TO 440 LB (220 KG)

SIBERIAN TIGER
LENGTH: 11 FT (3.3 M) HEAD TO TAIL TIP
WEIGHT: UP TO 660 LB (300 KG)

LARGEST CAT
A powerful, heavily muscled predator, the **SIBERIAN TIGER** uses stalk-and-ambush tactics to bring down large prey, such as deer, single-handedly.

LARGEST LAND CARNIVORE
The **KODIAK BROWN BEAR** uses its large size to intimidate other large predators. Although battles are rare, its massive strength and size usually results in it winning any violent conflicts.

GIRAFFE
HEIGHT: 18 FT (5.5 M)
WEIGHT: 1.4 TONS

LARGEST LAND MAMMAL
An angry or frightened **AFRICAN ELEPHANT** can bulldoze anything in its path. A single tusk can reach 10 ft (3 m) long.

ELEPHANT SEAL
LENGTH: 20 FT (6 M)
WEIGHT: 4 TONS

AFRICAN ELEPHANT
HEIGHT: 13 FT (4 M)
WEIGHT: UP TO 6.3 TONS

LARGEST SEAL
A well-fed male **ELEPHANT SEAL** is as heavy as a real elephant. Dominant males, known as "beachmasters," fight fiercely to defend their territories.

TALLEST LAND MAMMAL
The muscular neck of the **GIRAFFE** is as long as a human is tall, and can be swung around like a battering ram to bash predators.

39

INDEX

Entries in **bold** refer to main subject entries; entries in *italics* refer to illustrations.

acorn woodpecker 27, *27*
adders 37, *37*
African bullfrog 18, *18*
African elephant 39, *39*
African foam grasshopper 14, *14*
alligators 12, *12*
anemones 22
anole lizards 25, *25*
anteaters 8, *8*
antelopes 20, *20*
ants 22, 22–3, 27, 28, 35
apes 26, *26*, 38, *38*
aphids 23, *22–3*
armadillos 14, *14*
armor 14
army ants 28, *28*

babies 11, **30–1**
basilisk lizard 7, *7*
bats 9, *9*
bears 8, 12, *12*, 38, *38*
beavers 33, *33*
bee-eaters 25, *25*
bees 9
beetles 8, *8*, 11, 35, *35*
bipedal walking 6
bite power 35
blue whale 38, *38–9*
bodily fluids **10–11**, 14, 15
brine shrimp 16, *16*
brood parasites 23
Bryde's whale 18, *18*
building **32–3**
bullfrogs 18, *18*
butterflies *30*, 33

camouflage 15, **36–7**
caterpillars 22, *22*, 30, *30*
Chacoan horned frog 37, *37*
chameleons 16, *16*
cheetahs 20, *20*
chimps 26, *26*
clams 14, 17, *17*
clownfish 22, *22*
cockchafer beetle 8, *8*
courtship displays **24–5**
cowbirds 23
crabs 14, 27, 28, *28*
cuckoos 23, *23*

dead-leaf mantis 15, *15*
dippers 7
dolphins 27, *27*
droppings 10, 11
dung beetles 11, 35, *35*

eagles 9
ears 9, 21, *21*
Egyptian vulture 26, *26*
elephants 17, *17*, 21, *21*, 34, *34*, 39, *39*
elephant seals 39, *39*
European bee-eater 25, *25*
excrement 10, 11, 35, 35

feeding 10, 11, *11*, **18–19**, 22, 23, *23*, 30, 31, *31*
finches 26
flying frogs 7, *7*
foam-nest tree frog 11, *11*
food storage 19
frogs 7, *7*, 11, *11*, 18, *18*, 37, *37*

Gaboon viper 13, *13*
geckos 36, *36*
gerenuk antelopes 20, *20*
giant anteater 8, *8*
giant panda 30, *30*
giant tortoise 17
giraffes 21, *21*, 39, *39*
gliding 7
glowworms 24, *24*
gorilla, mountain 38, *38*
grasshoppers *14–15*, 15
great potoo 36, *36*
great white shark 35, *35*
greater frigate 24, *24*
grizzly bear 12, *12*

hares 24, *24*
harvest mouse 33, *33*
hearing, sense of 9, 21, *21*
hermit crabs 27
homes, animal **32–3**
honeybees 16, *16*
honeydew 23
honeyguides 23
hooded seal 25, *25*
horned lizards 10
hyenas 19

impalas 23, *23*
imperial moth 36, *36*
infrared light 9

jackals 19
jaguars 37
jumping spiders 9, *9*

kangaroos 21, *21*, 30, *30*, 38, *38*
kingfishers 7, *7*
koalas 30
kodiak brown bear 38, *38*
koi carp 17, *17*
komodo dragon 10, *10–11*

labord's chameleon 16, *16*
leaf-tail gecko 36, *36*
lemurs 6, *6*, 20, *20*
leopards 19, *19*, 37
leopard seal 19, *19*
life span **16–17**
lions 13, *13*, 37, 37
lizards 7, *7*, 10, *10*, 16, *16*, 25, *25*
locusts 29, *29*

macaws 17, *17*
mantises 15, *15*
marsupial mammals 30, 38, *38*
masked weaver bird 33, *33*
mayflies 16, *16*
metamorphosis 30

mice 33, *33*
migrations 28
moths 9, 36, *36*
mountain gorillas 38, *38*
movement **6–7**
mudskippers 6, *6*

nests 33, *33*

octopuses 27, *27*
opossums 15, *15*, 30
ostriches 38, *38*
oxpeckers 23, *23*

pandas 30, *30*
pangolins 14
parasite–host situation **22–3**
parrots 17, *17*
peacock katydid *14–15*, 15
peacocks 25, *25*
penguins 7
pheromones 8
piranhas 9, 29
polar bear 8
possums 30
prairie dogs 32
problem solving 27
proboscis monkey 21, *21*
pus 10

quahog clam 17, *17*

red crabs 28, *28*
red kangaroo 38, *38*
rhinos 9
ring-tailed lemur 20, *20*
ruffs 24, *24–5*

sailfish 7
scavengers 10, 19
sea anemones 22
seabirds 10
sea cucumber 10
seals 19, *19*, 25, *25*, 30, *30–1*, 39, *39*
self-defense 10, **14–15**
senses **8–9**, 21, *21*
sharks 13, *13*, 35, *35*, 37
shells 14
shrimps 16, *16*
Siberian tiger 38, *38*
sidewinding adders 37, *37*
sifaka 6, *6*
sight 9
slime 10
smell, sense of 8, 21, *21*
snails 14
spiders 9, *9*
spit 10
Surinam toad 11
swimming 7
symbiotic relationships **22–3**

tadpoles 11, 30
tarsiers 21, *21*
termites 32, *32*
three-banded armadillo 14, *14*
tigers 21, *21*, 37, 38, *38*

tiger shark 13, *13*
tomato hornworm caterpillar 22, *22*
tools, using **26–7**
tortoises 17, *17*
T rex 35
turkey vultures 11, *11*

ultraviolet light 9
urine 10

veined octopus 27, *27*
vipers 13, *13*
Virginia opossum 15, *15*, 30
vomit 10
vultures 19, *19*, 27

wasp grubs 11, 22, *22*
weasels 34, *34*
weaver ant 27
weaver birds 33, *33*
whales 18, *18*, 38, *38–9*
white-backed vulture 19, *19*
whydahs 23
wild dogs 29, *29*
wolffish 12, *12*
wombats 30
woodpecker finch 26
woodpeckers 27, *27*